Mandalas

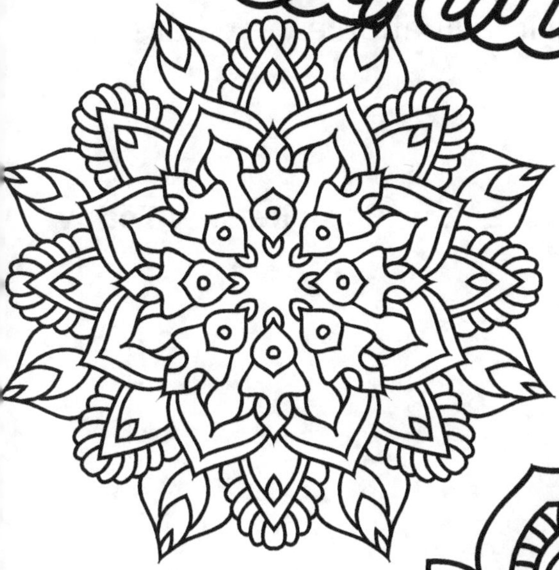

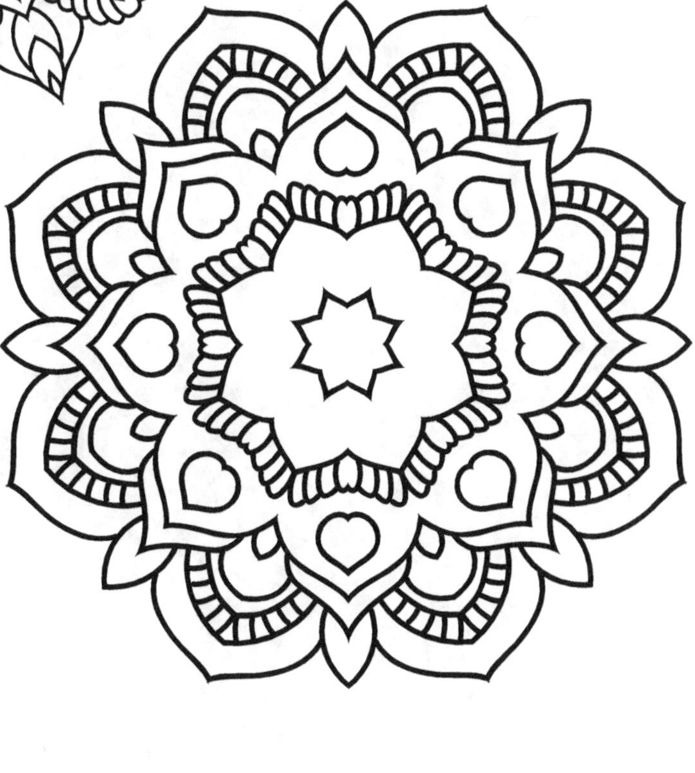

Thank you for being a part of this incredible journey with us. Together, we can inspire a lifelong love for reading and ignite the imagination everywhere.

Your Thoughts Matter! Share Your Book Review Today

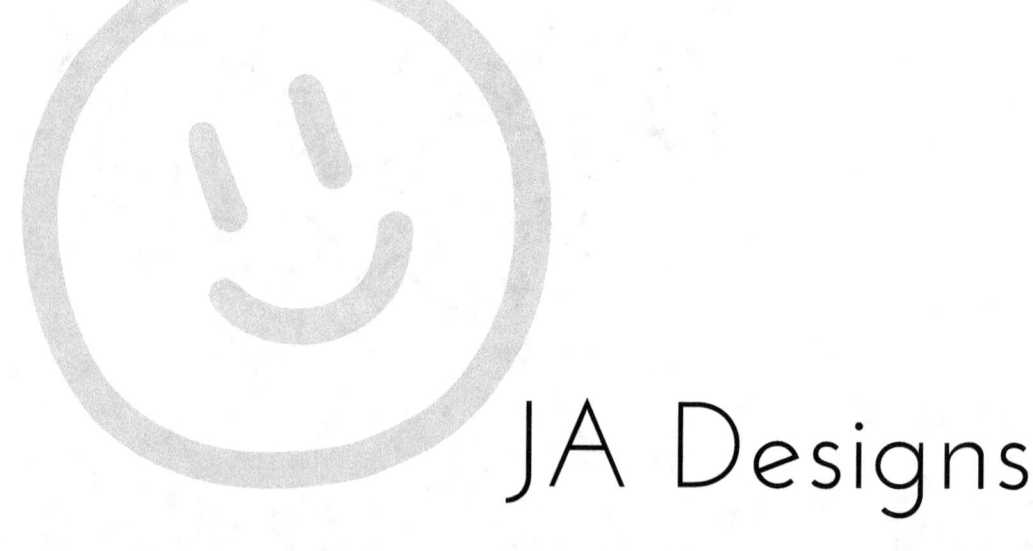

JA Designs

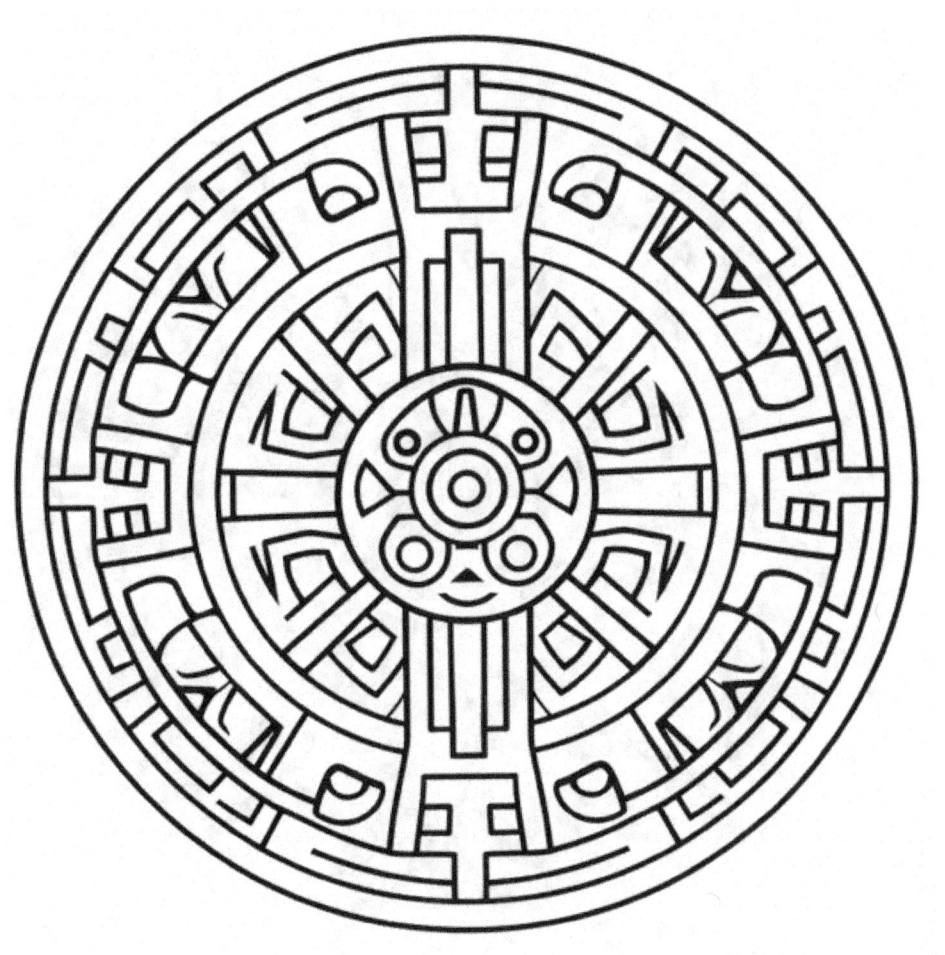

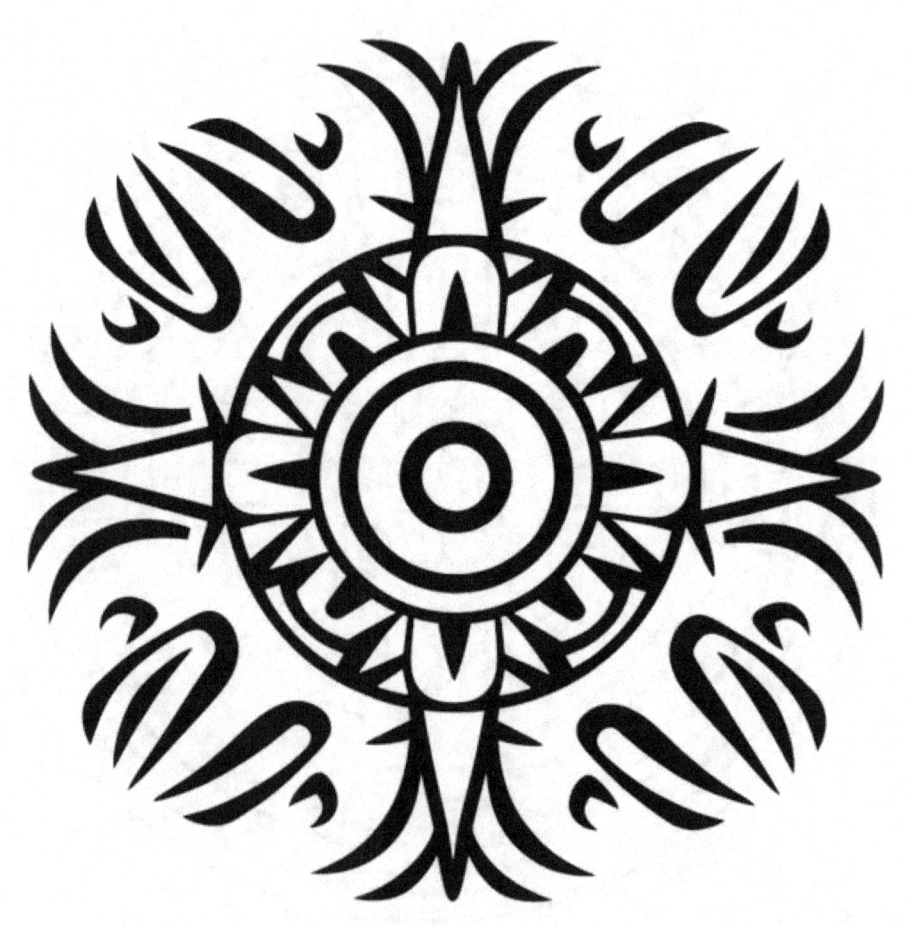

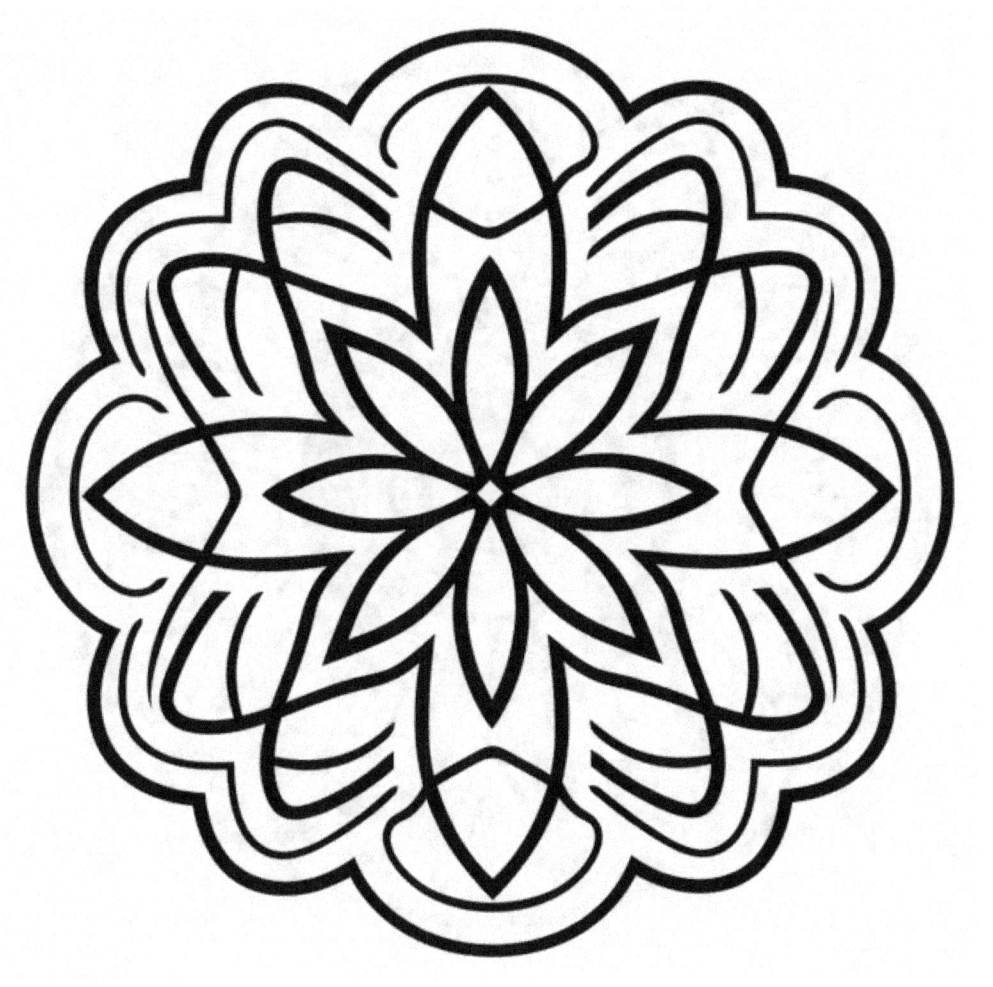

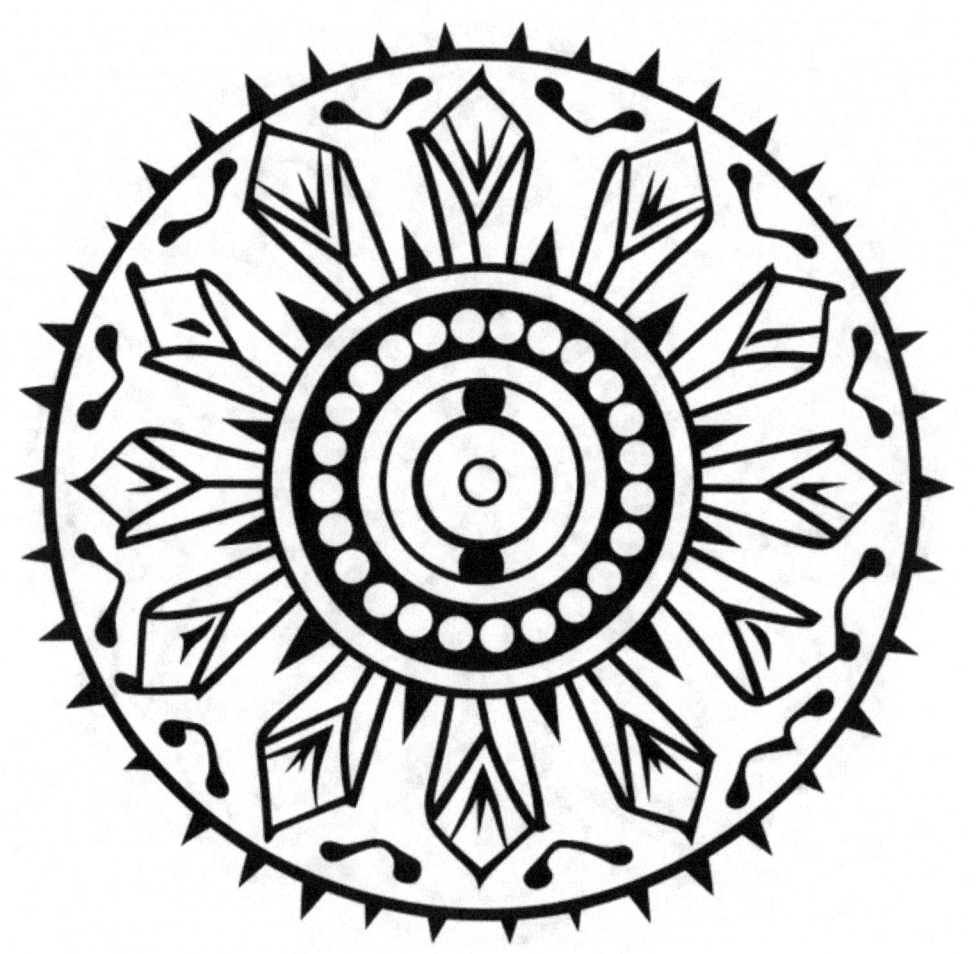

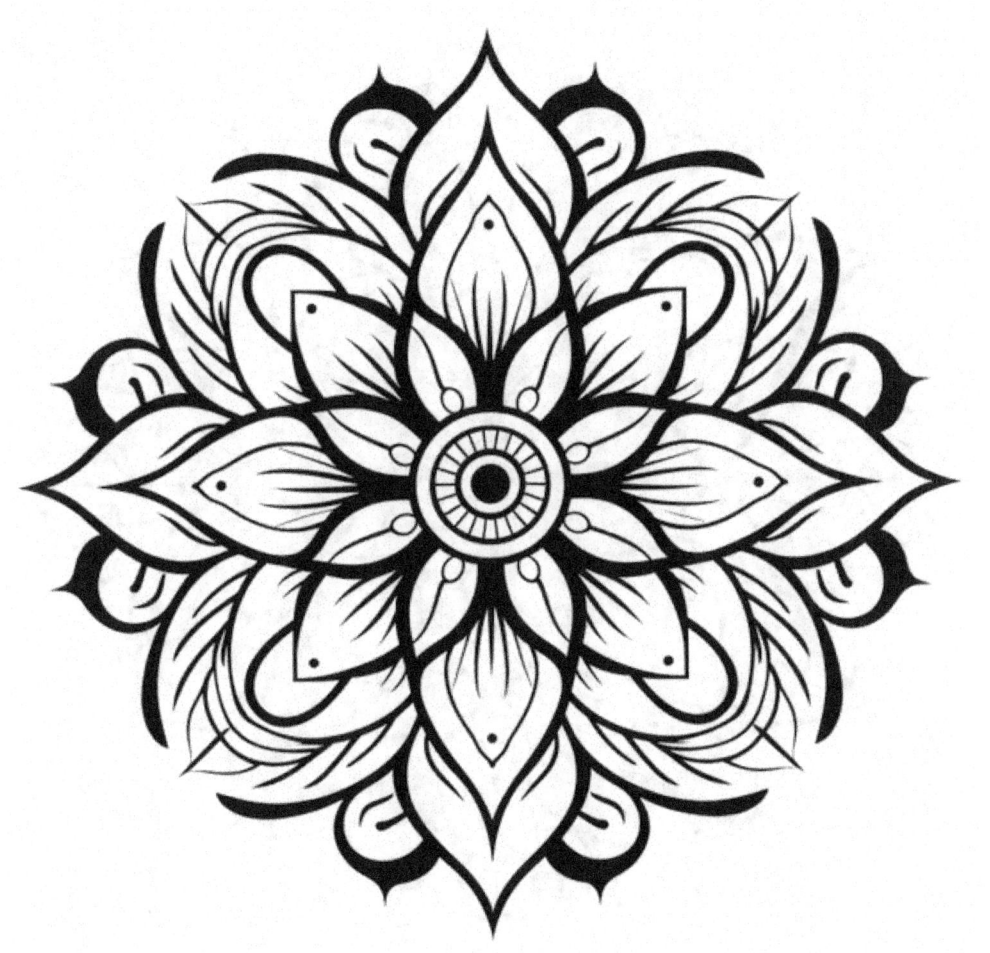

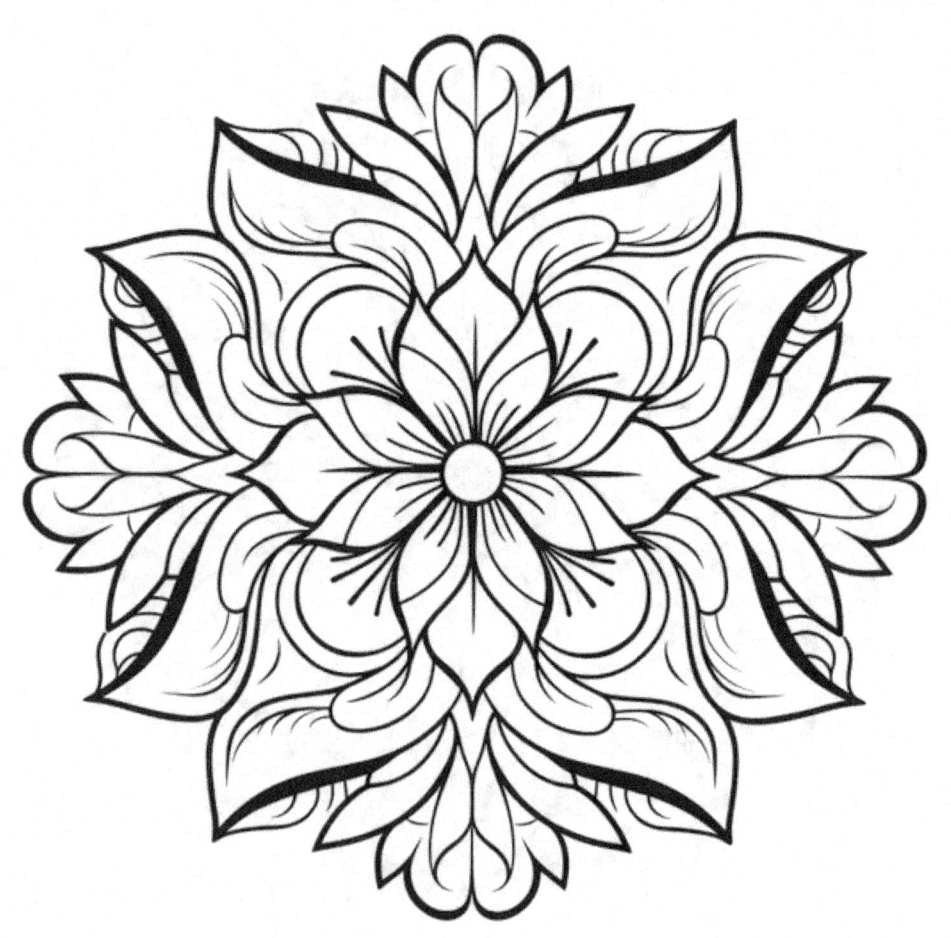

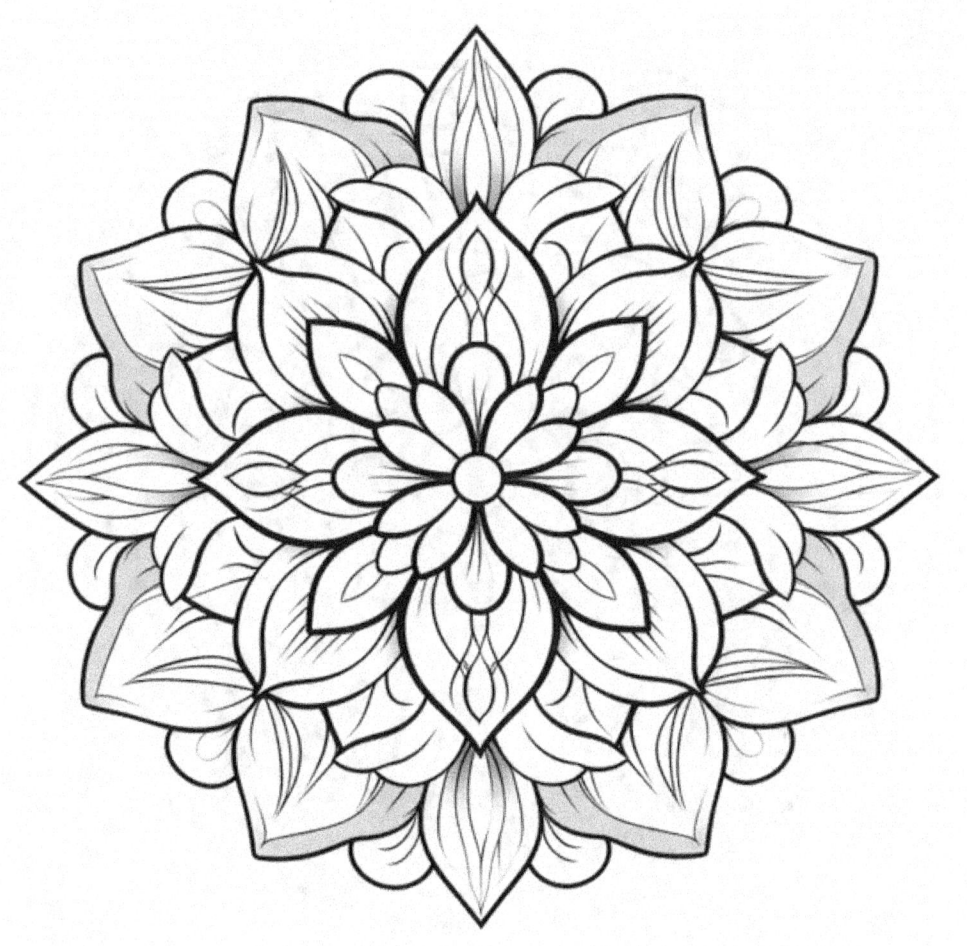

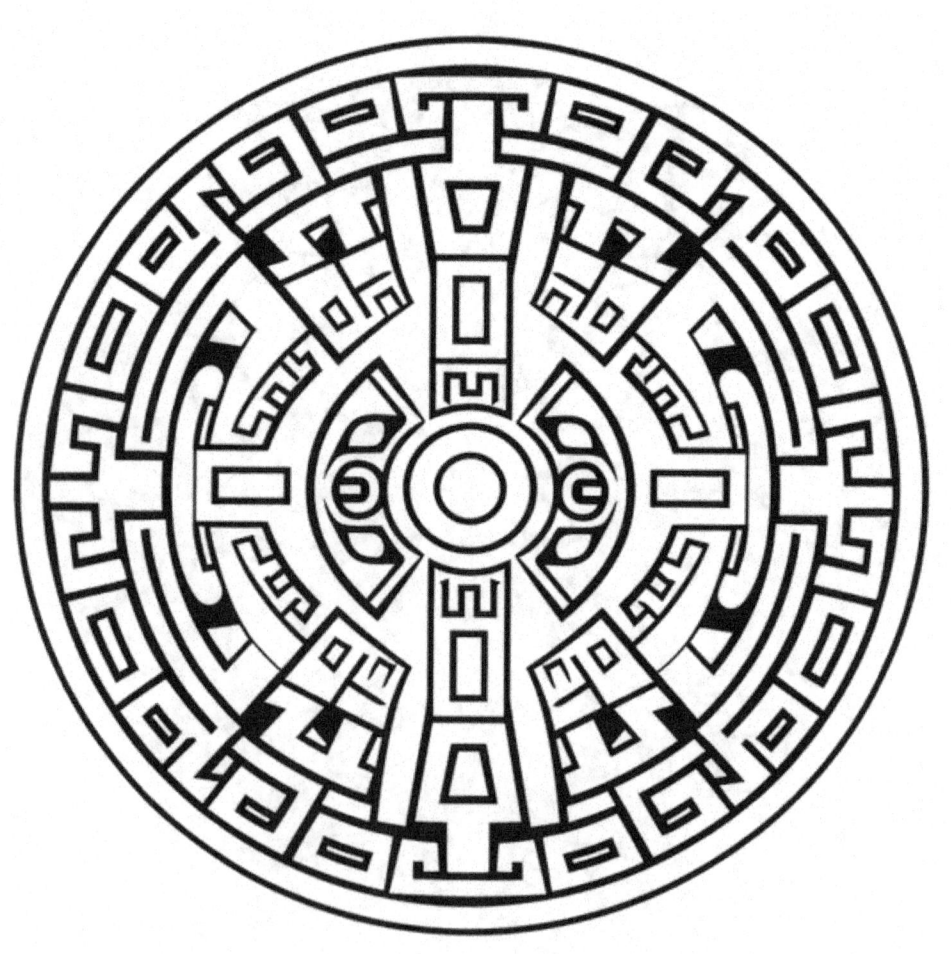

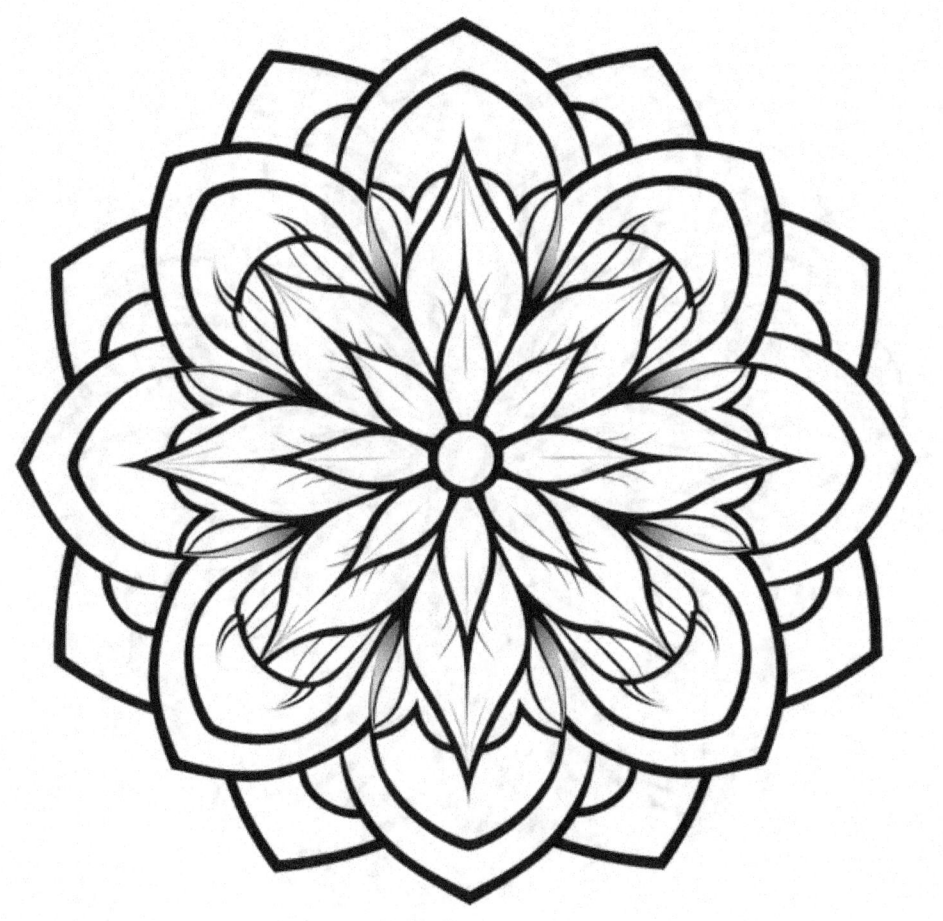

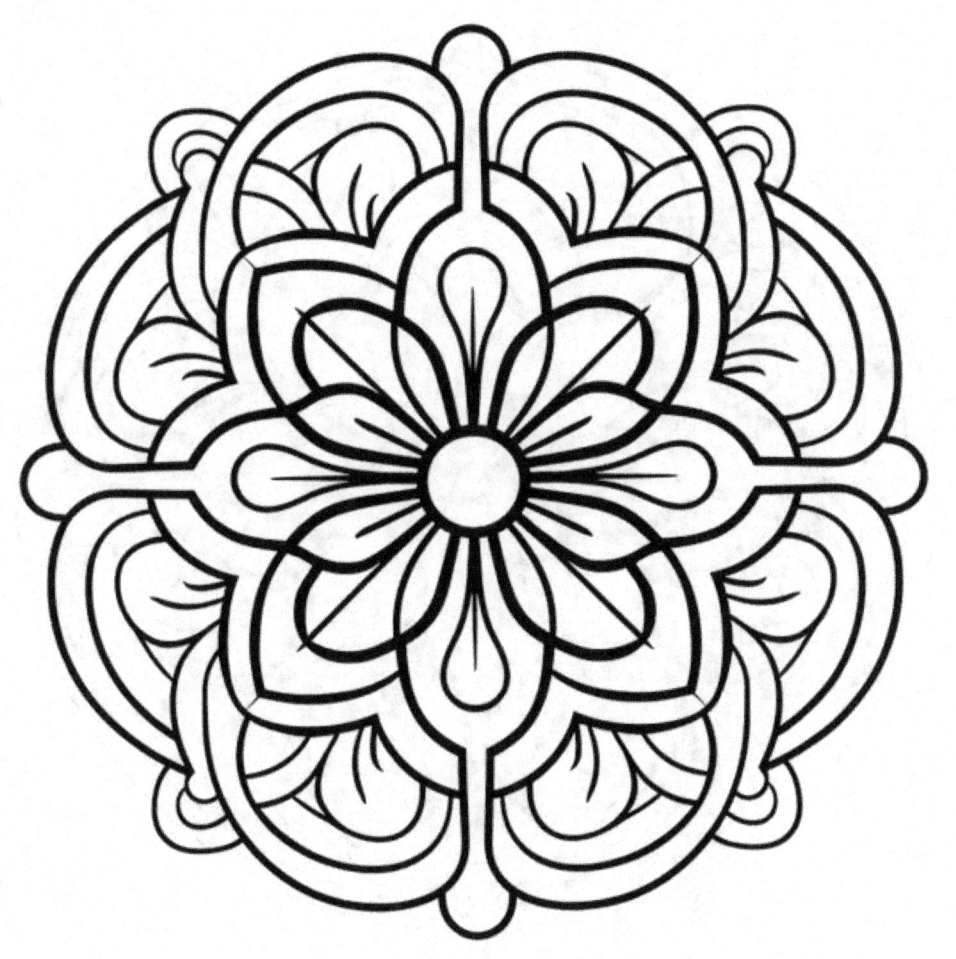

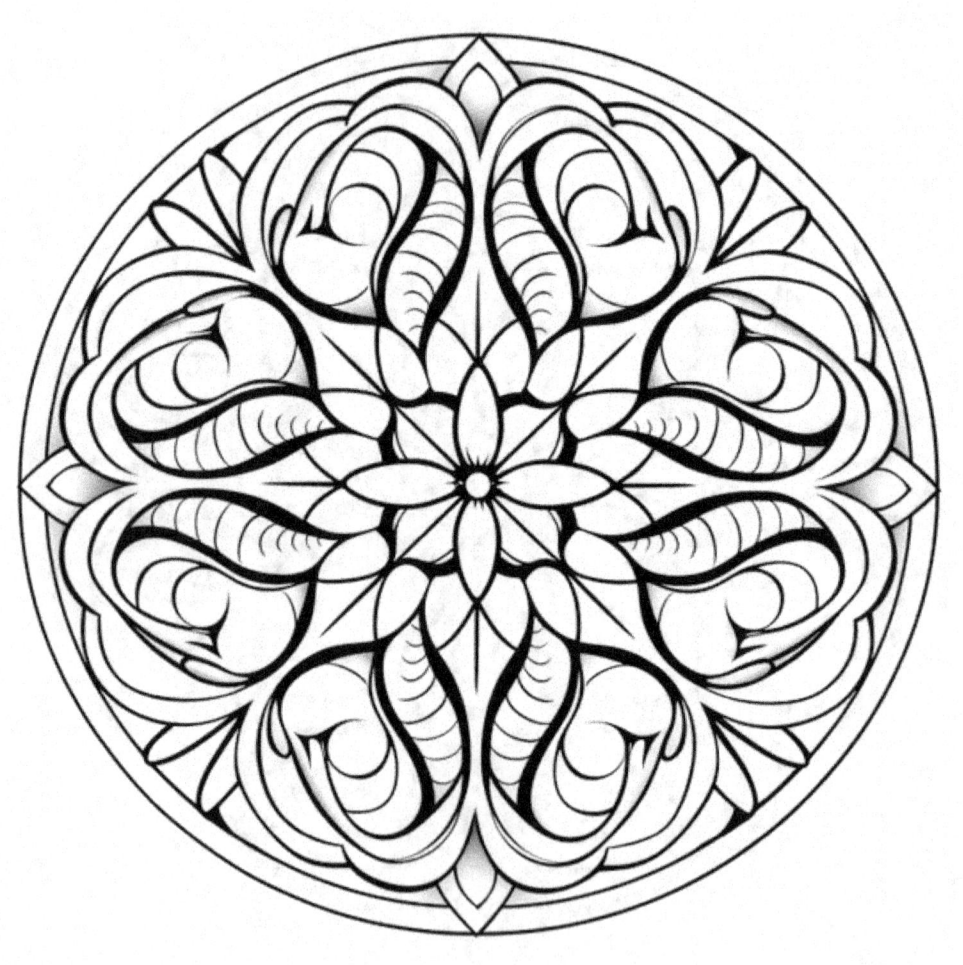

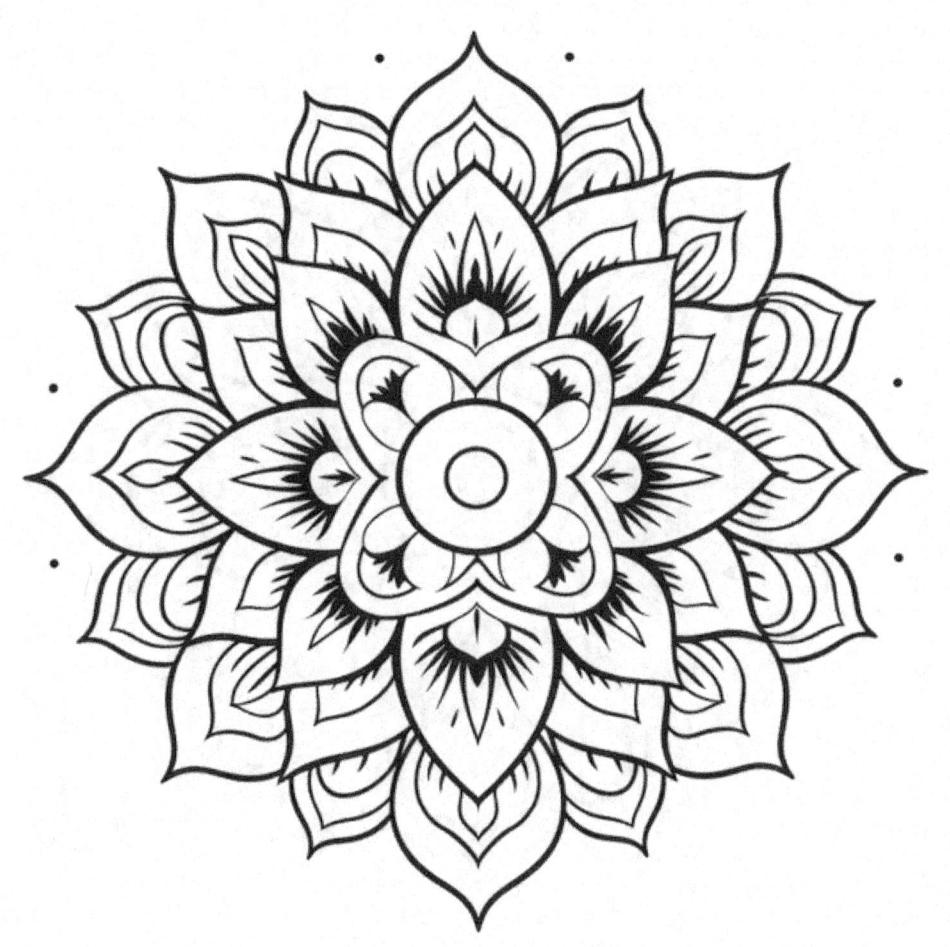

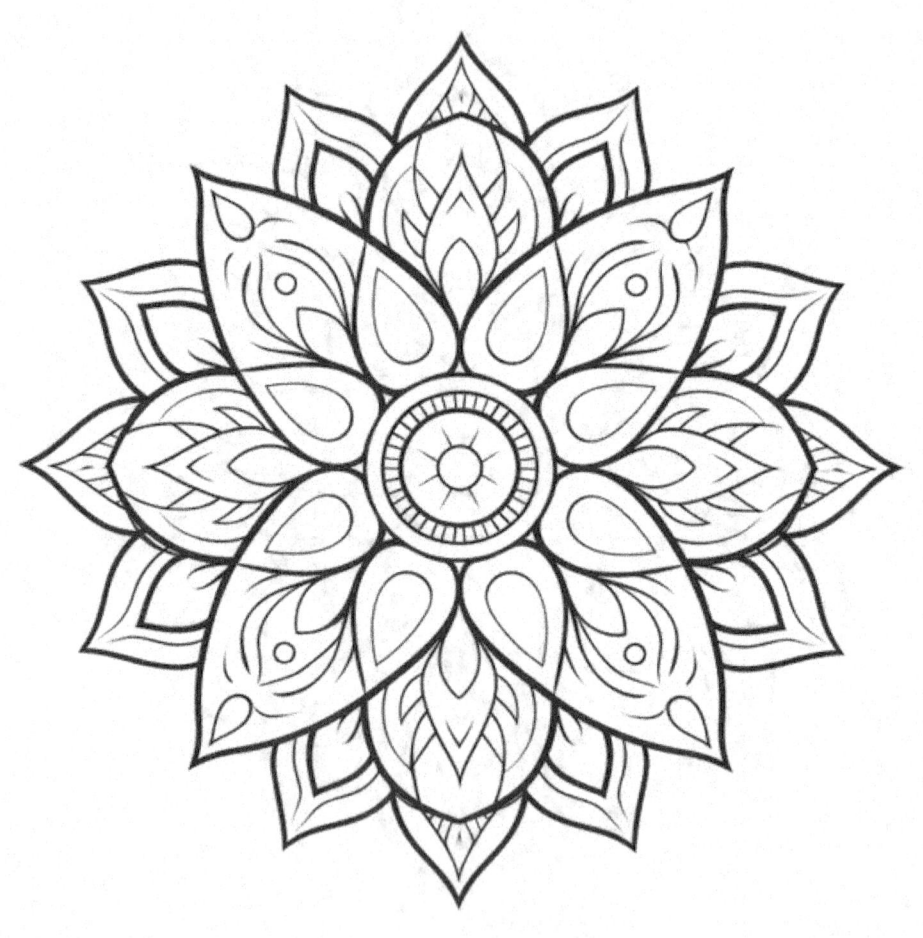

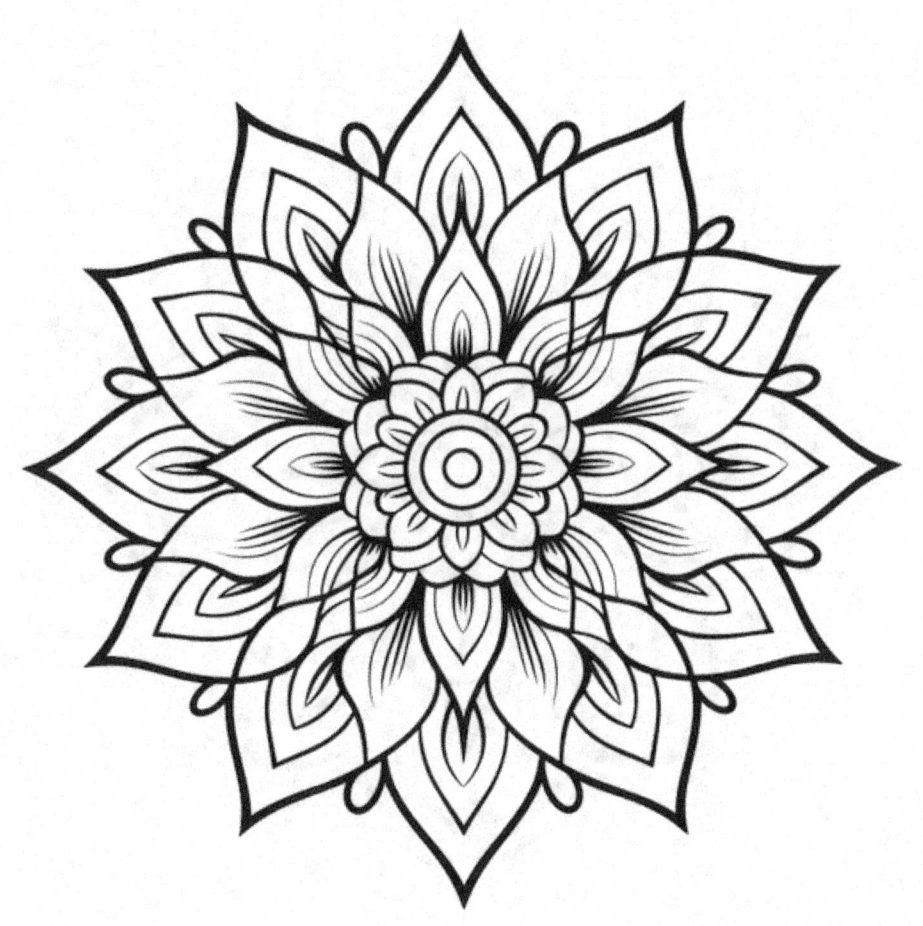

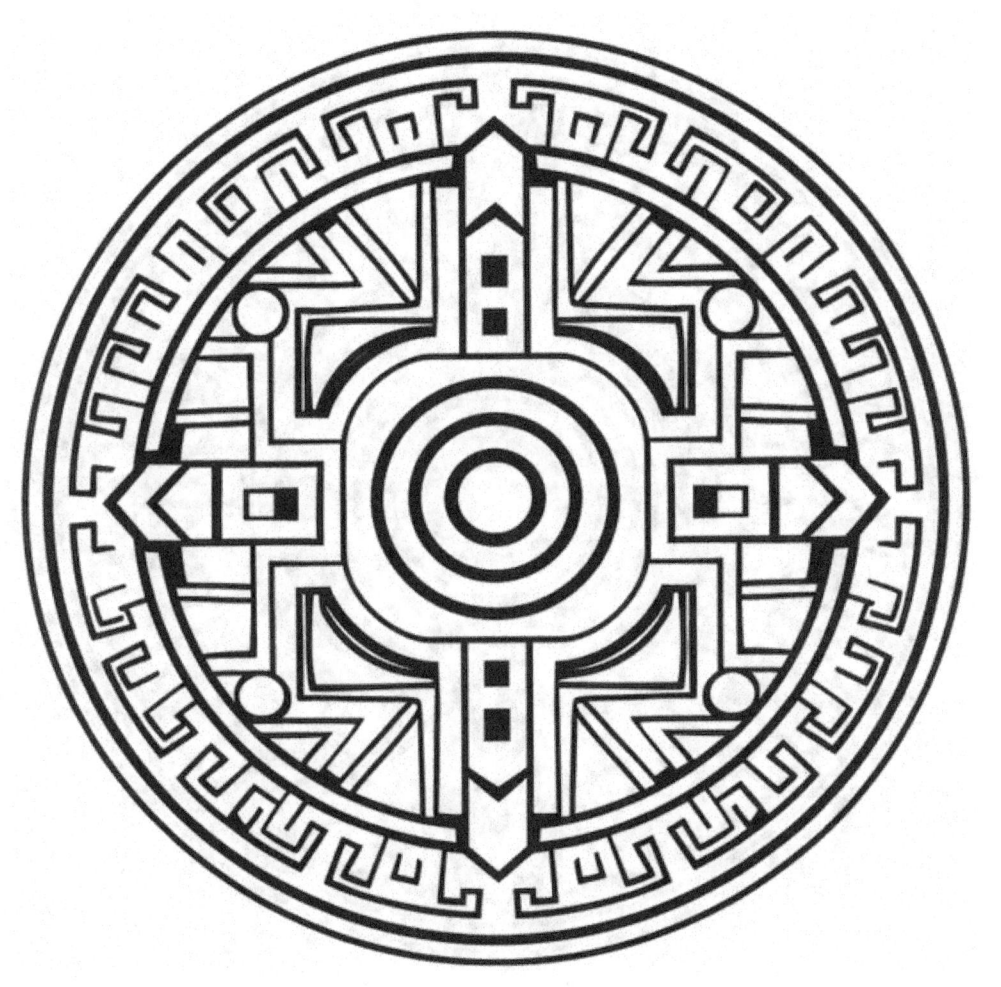

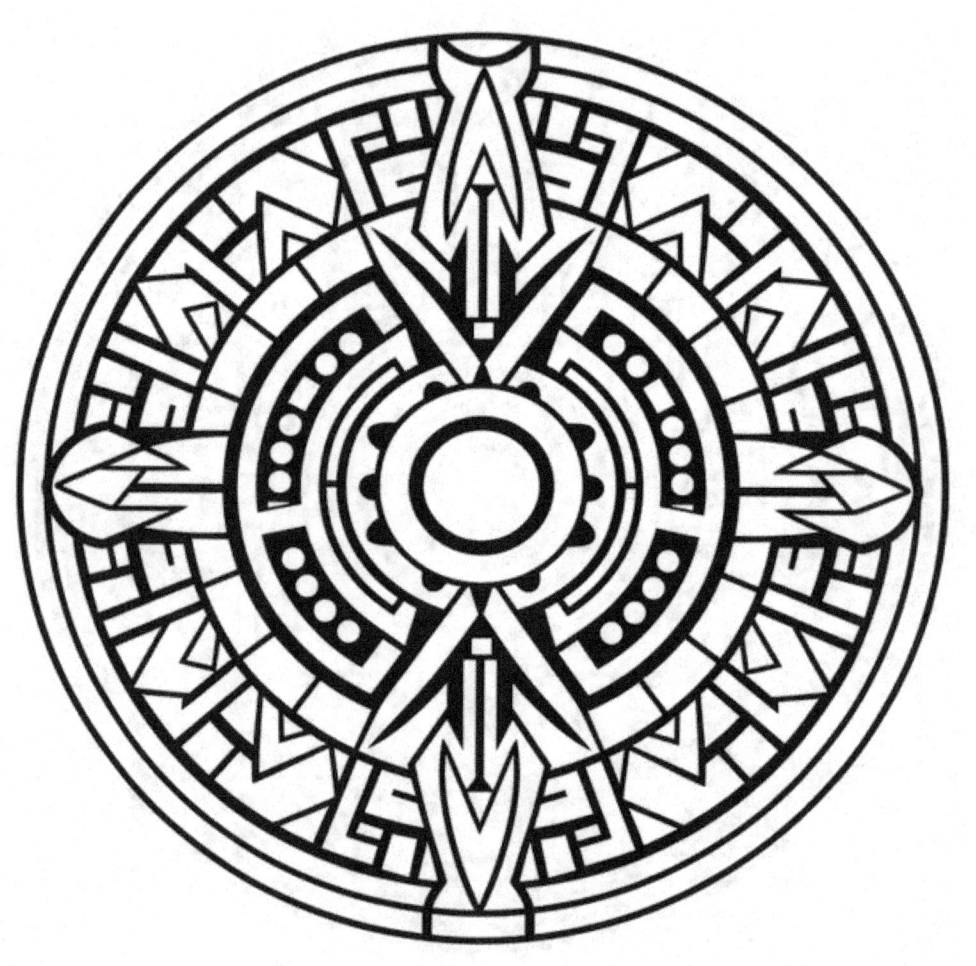

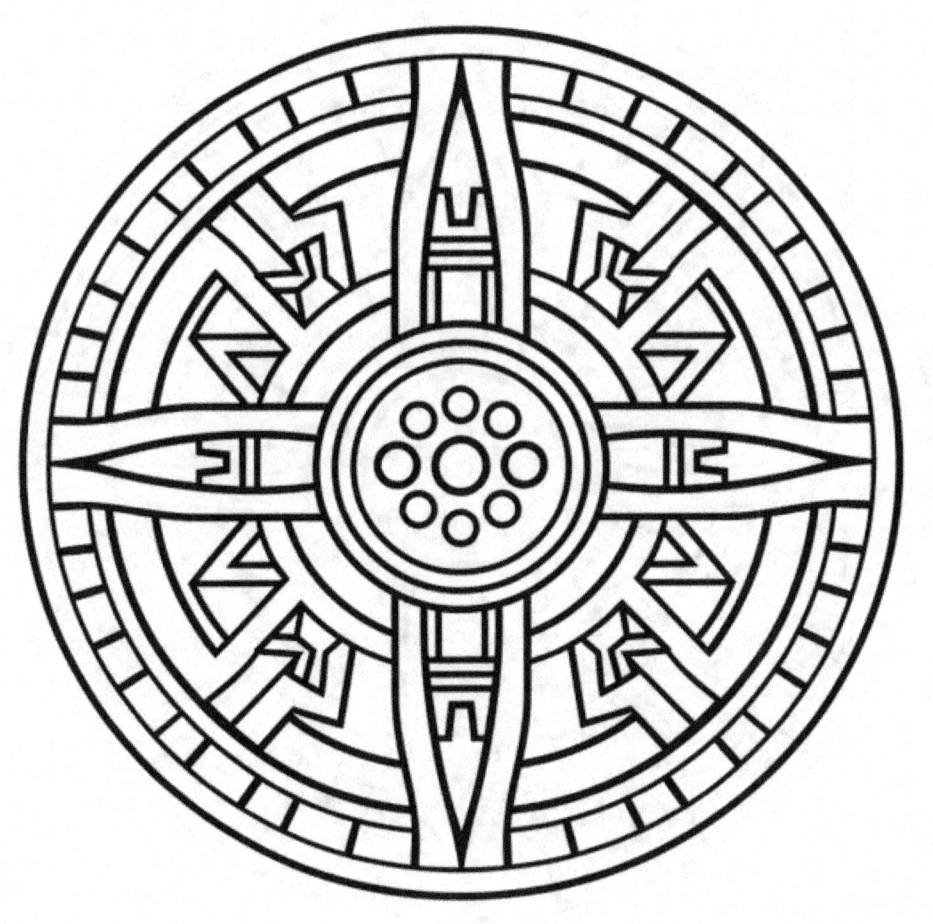

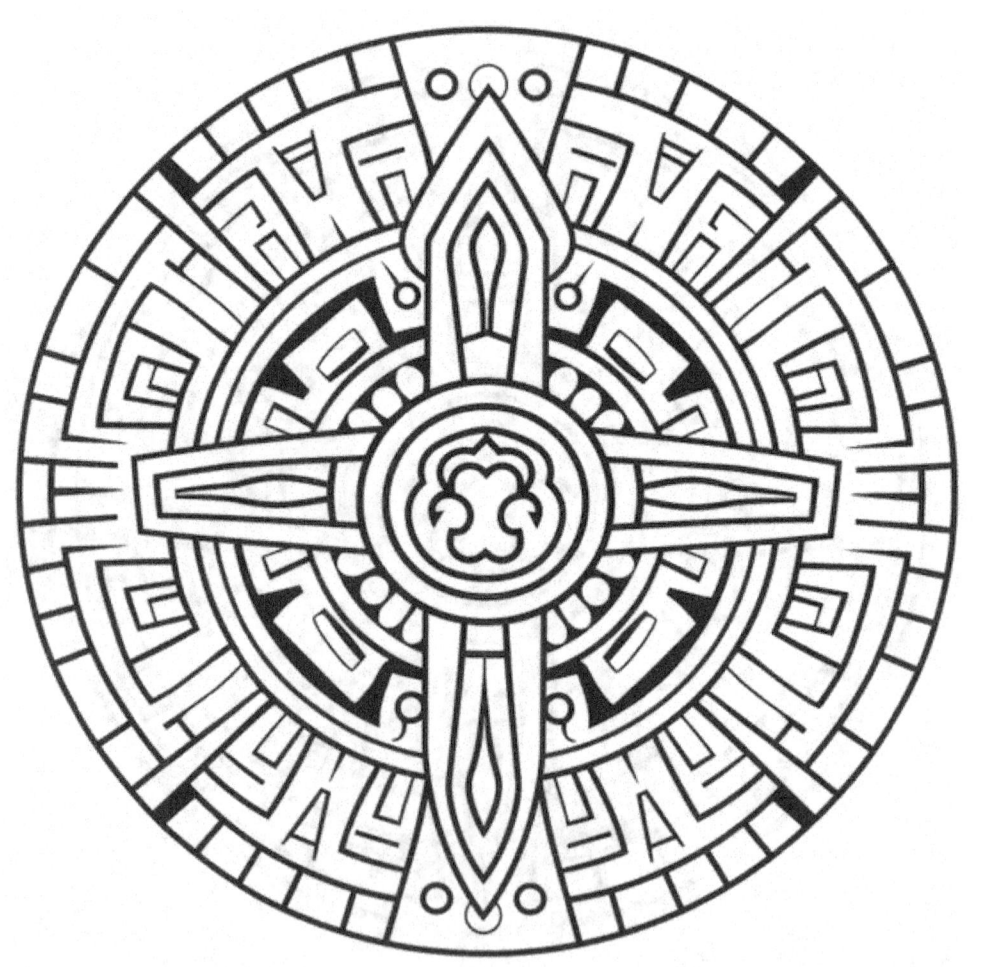

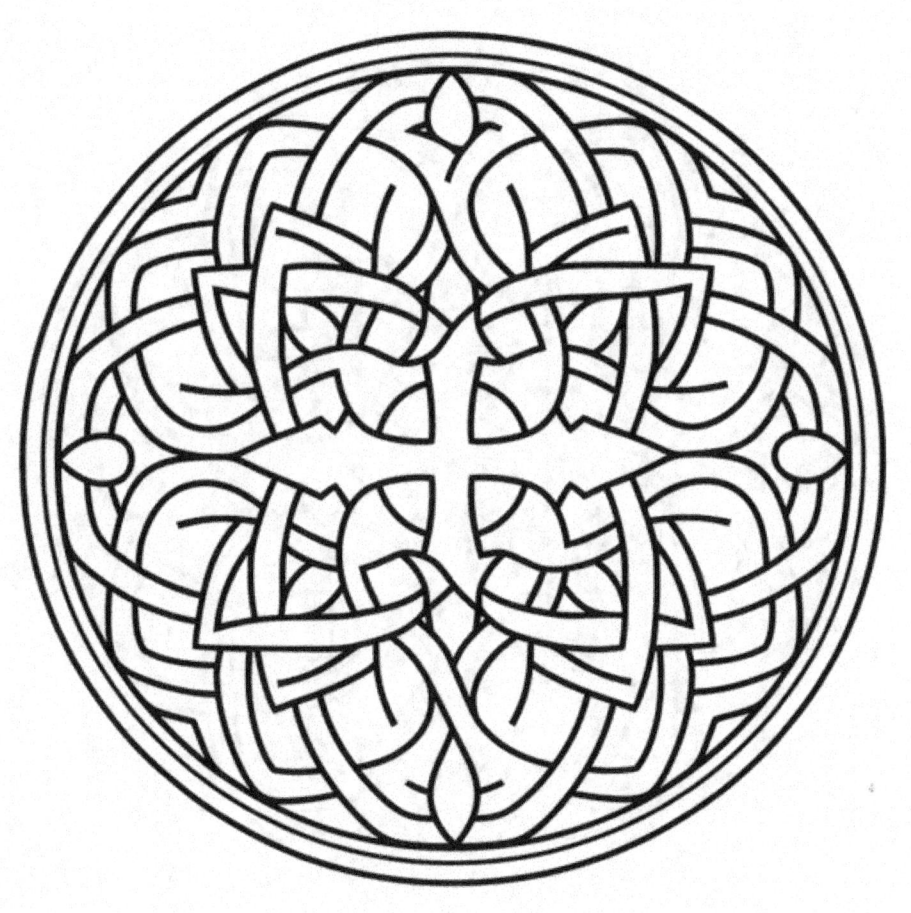

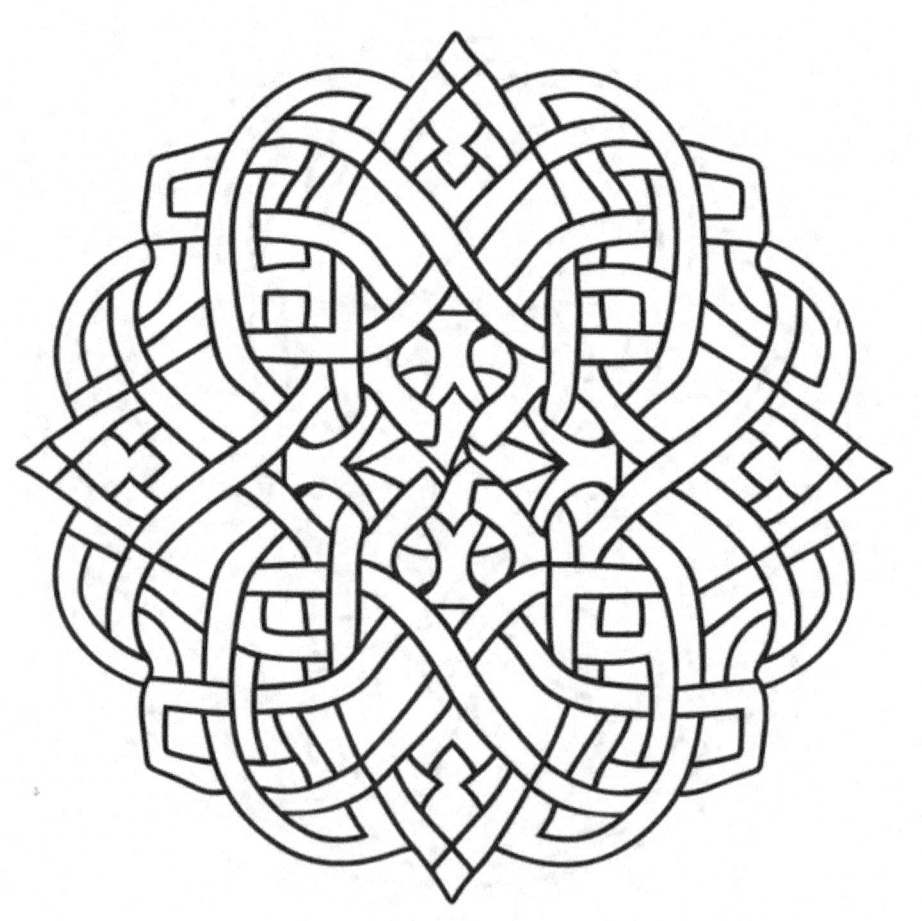

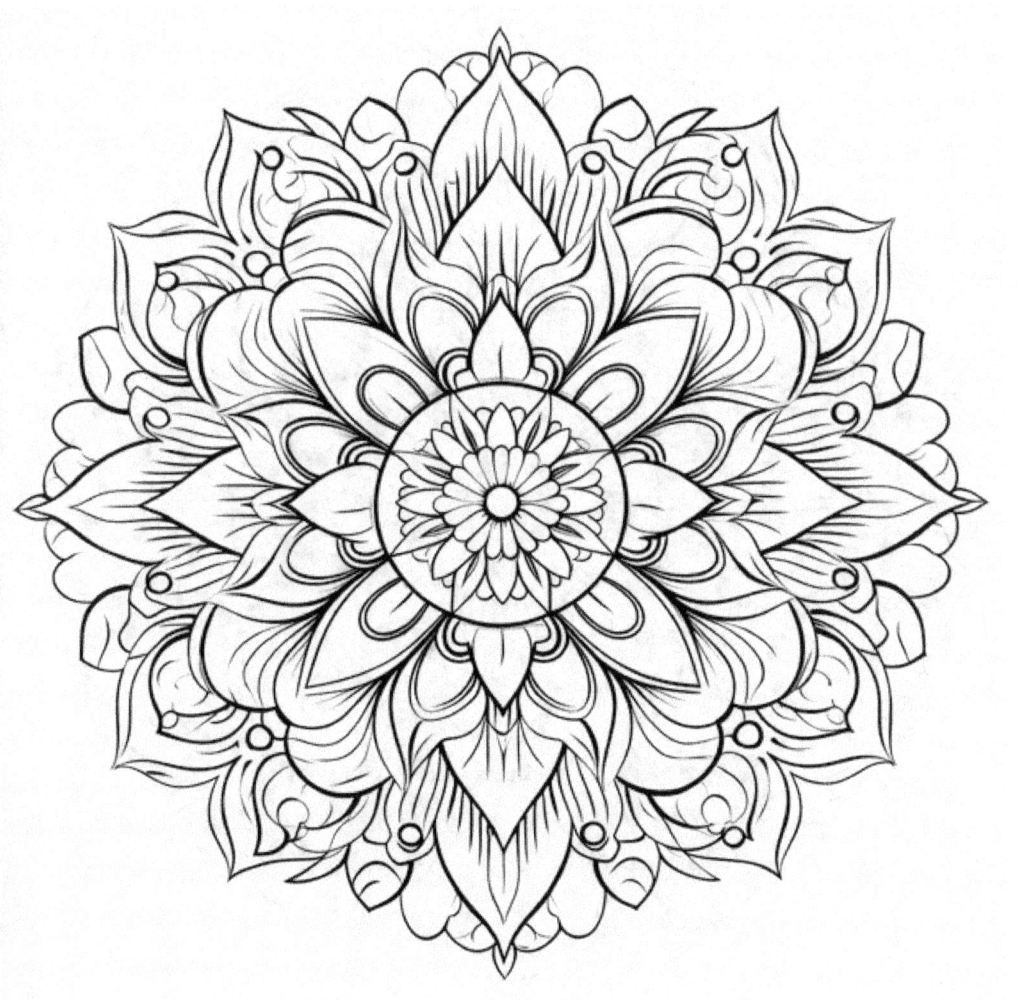

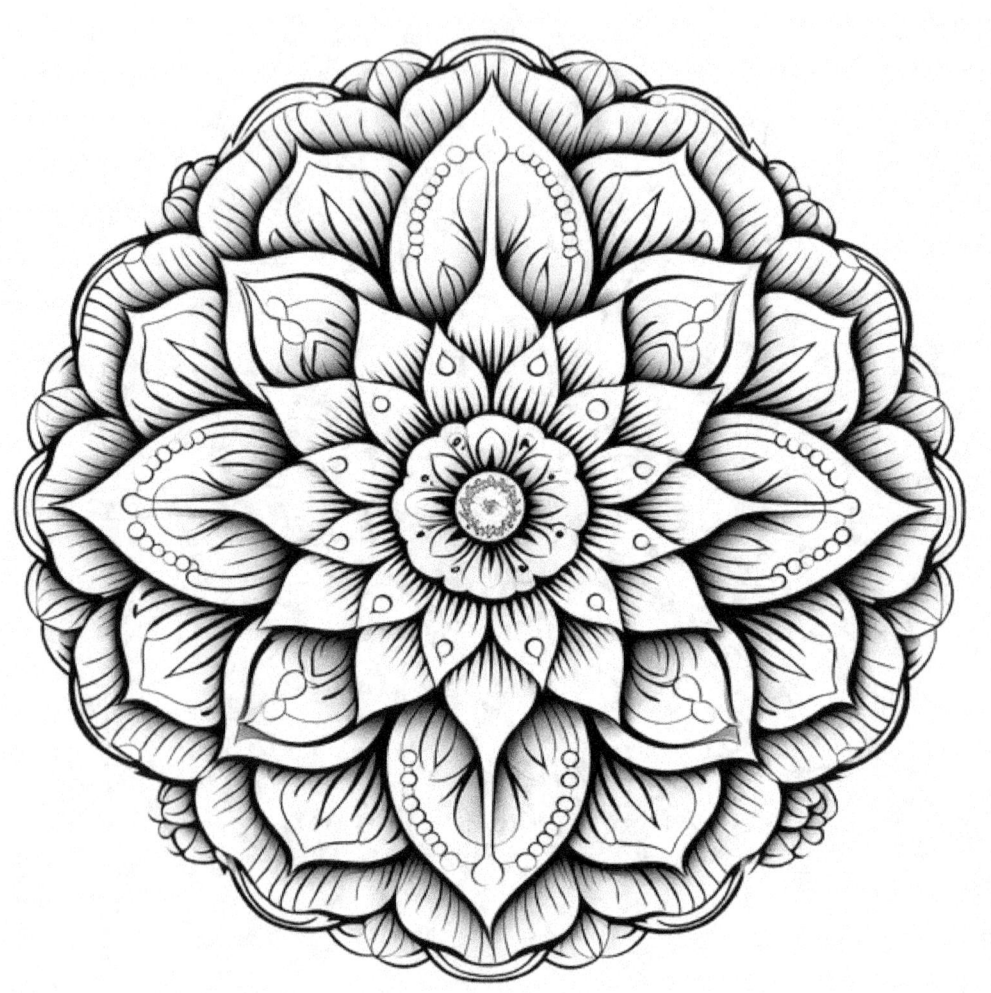

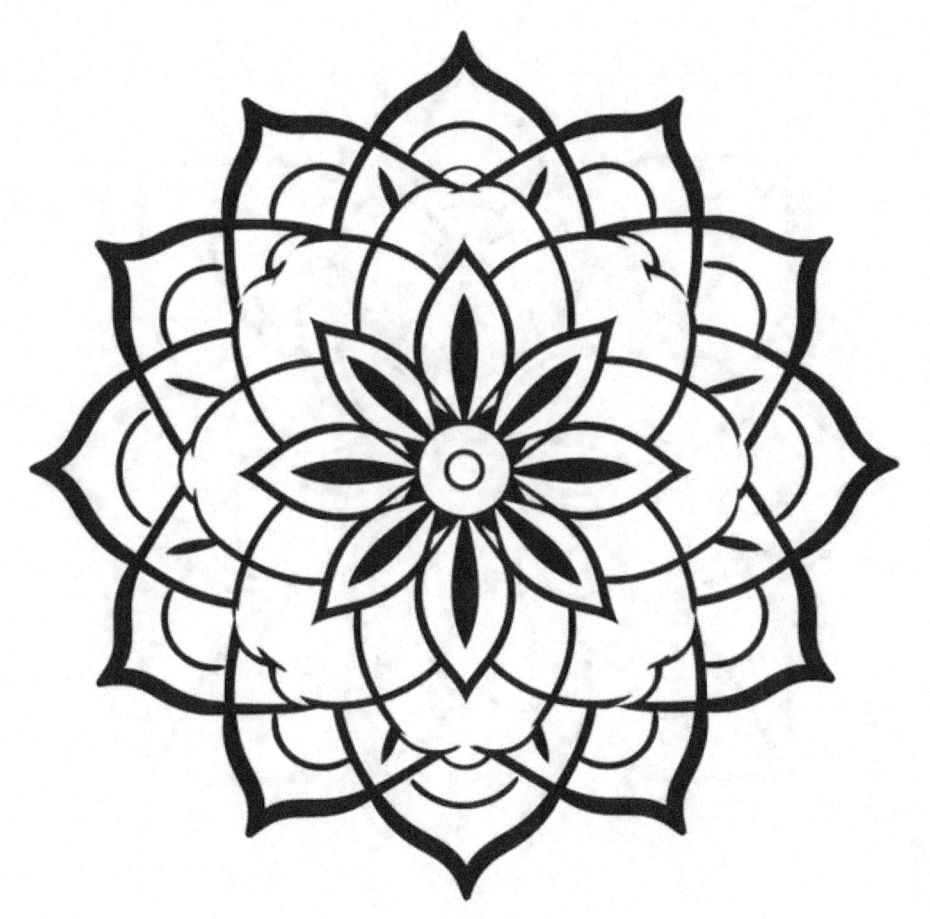

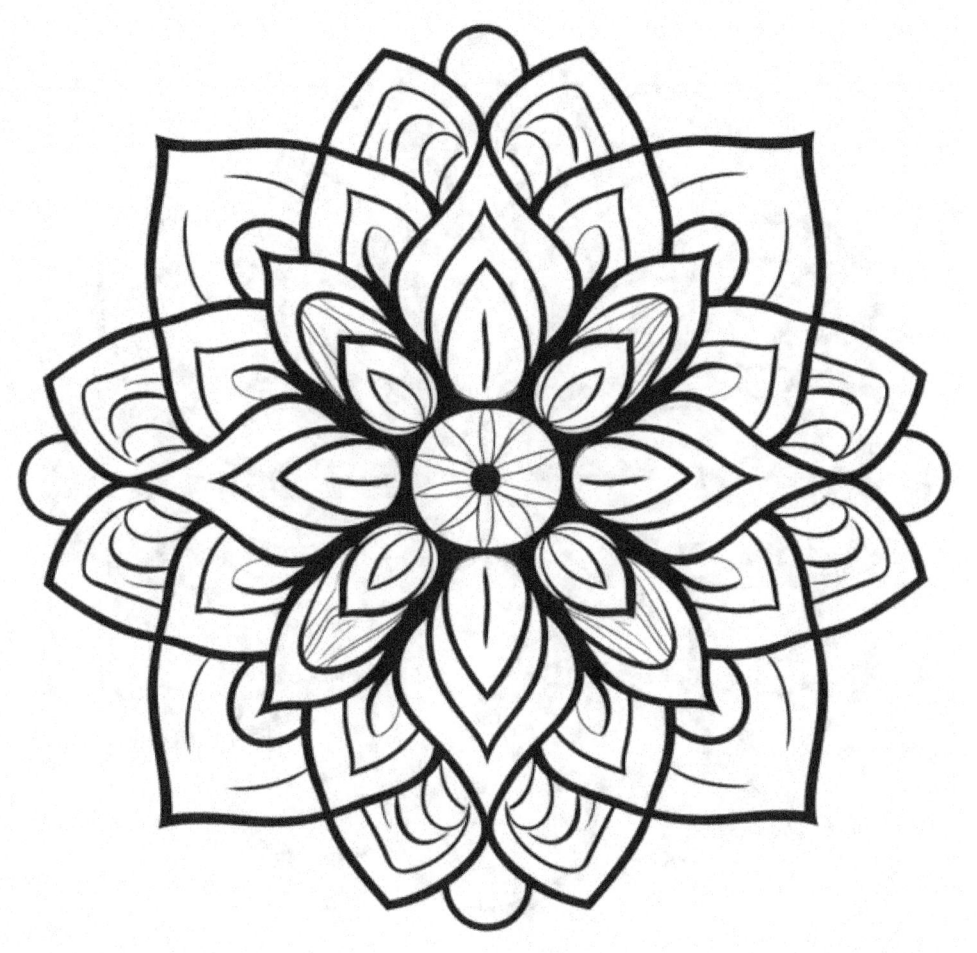

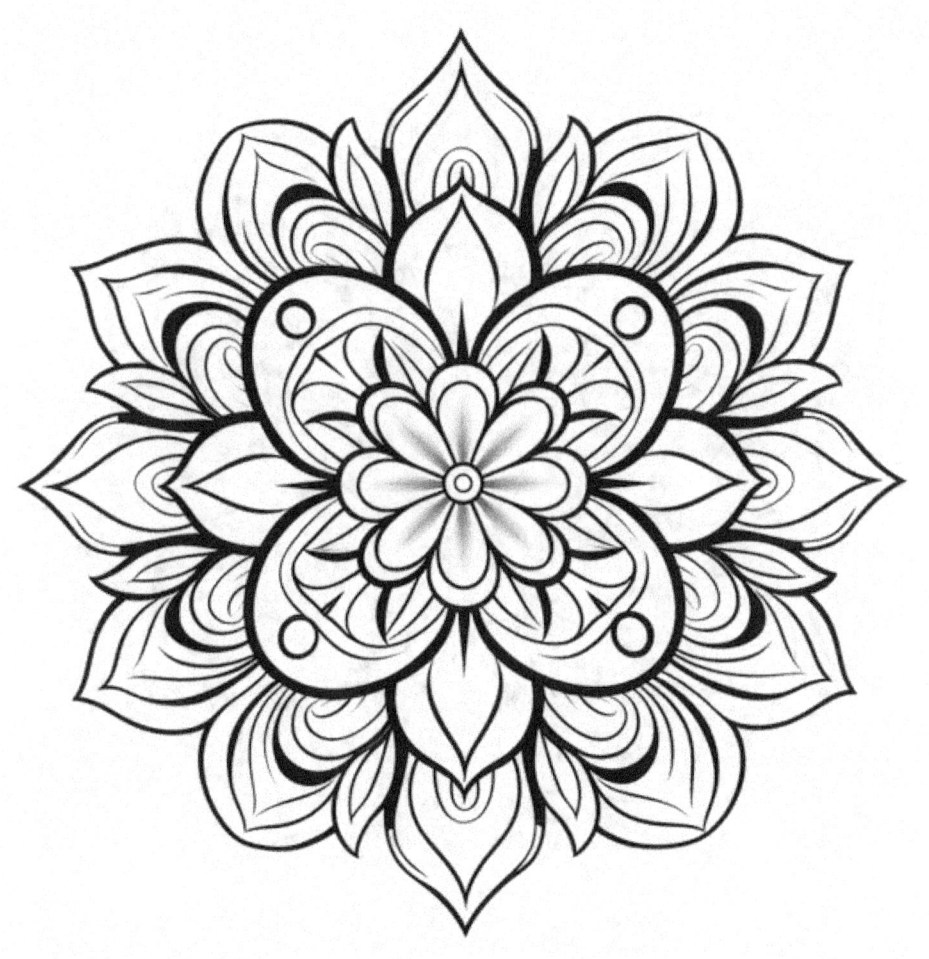

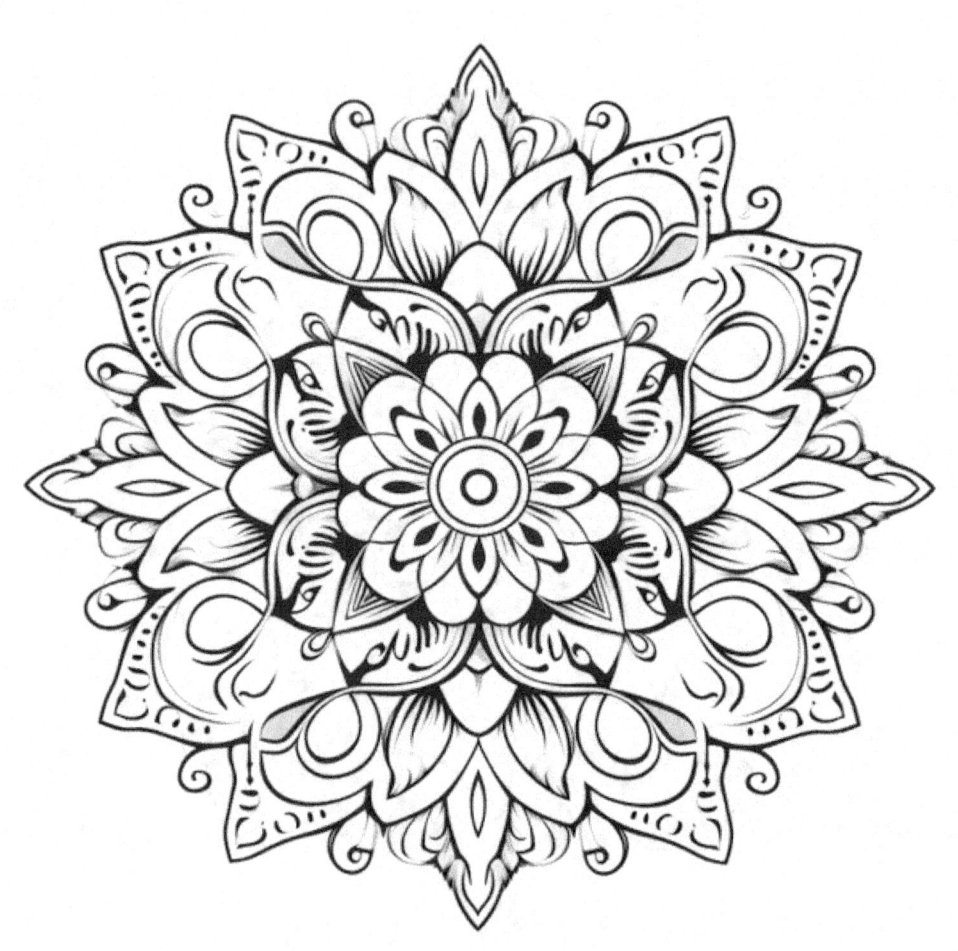

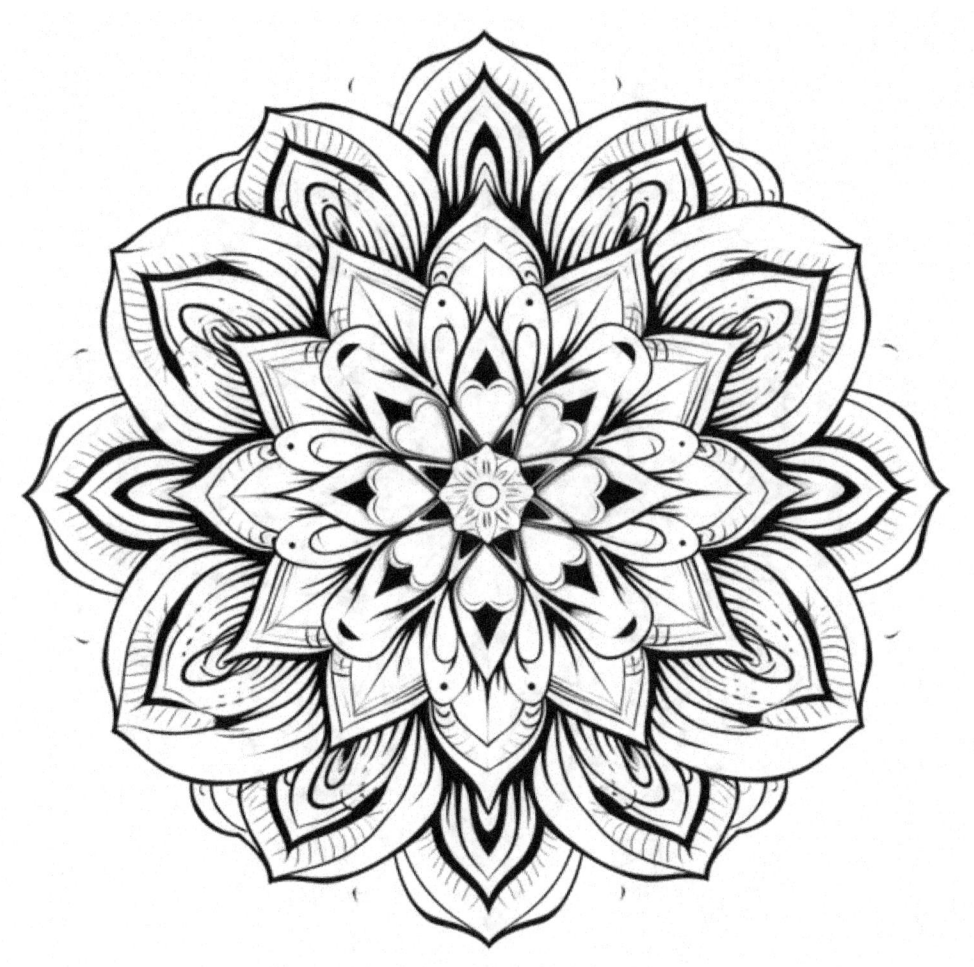

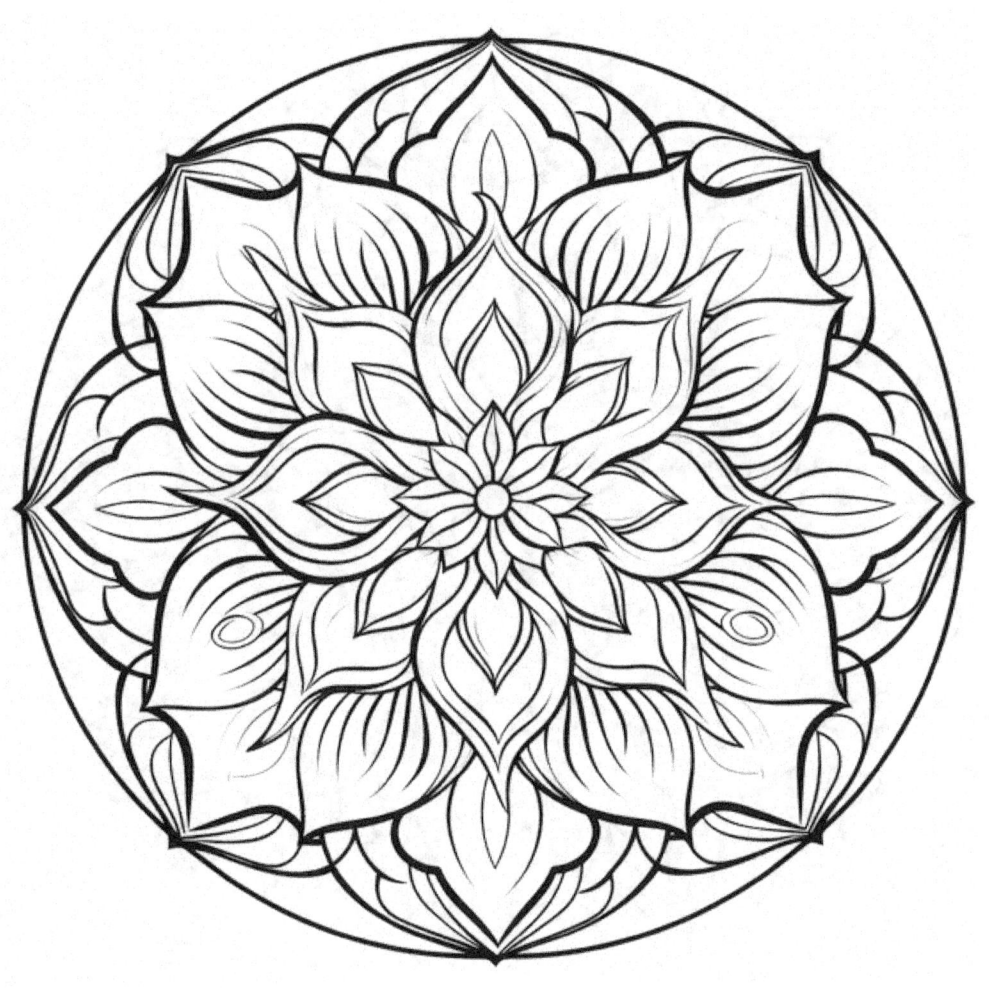

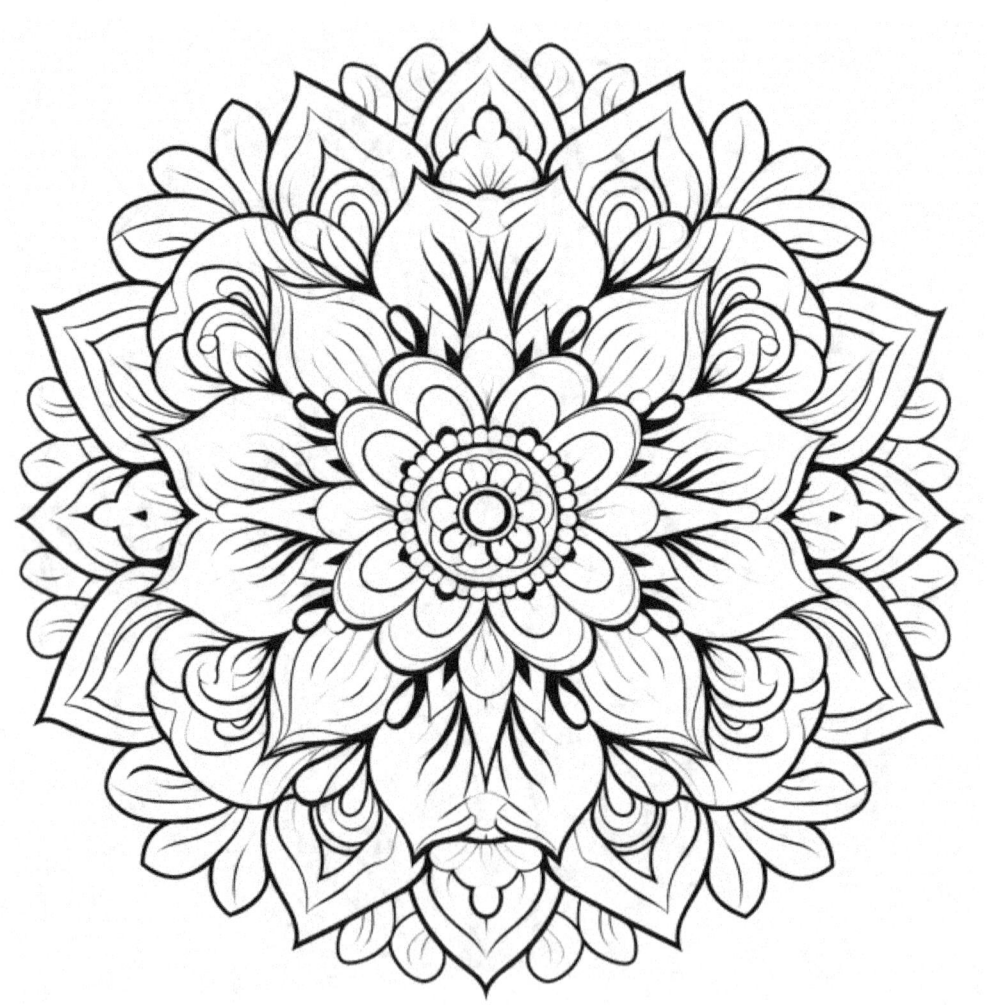

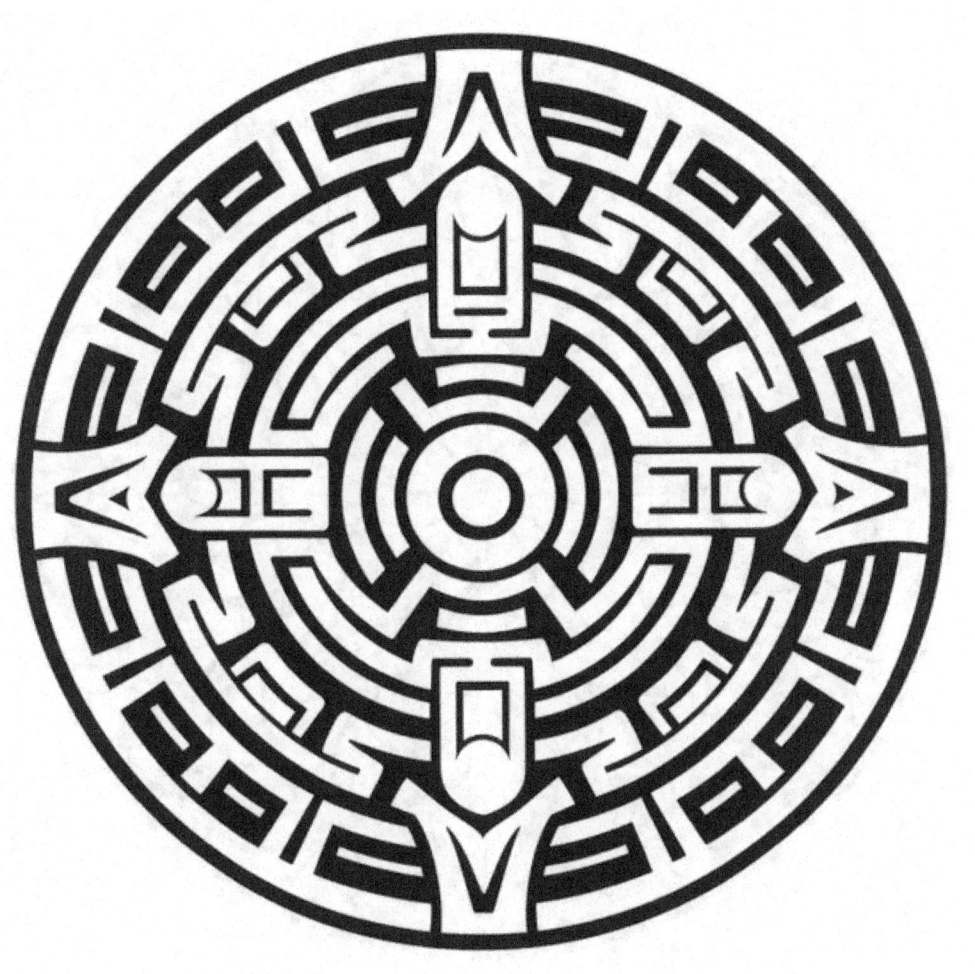

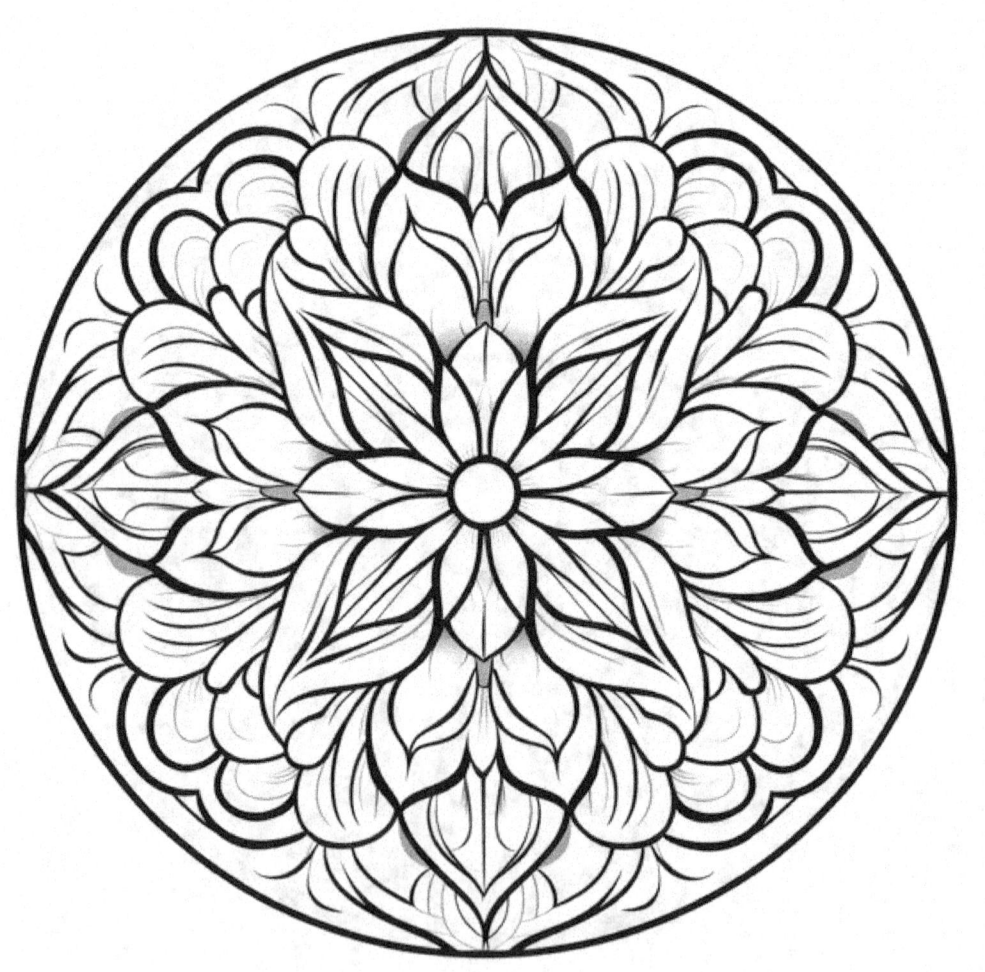

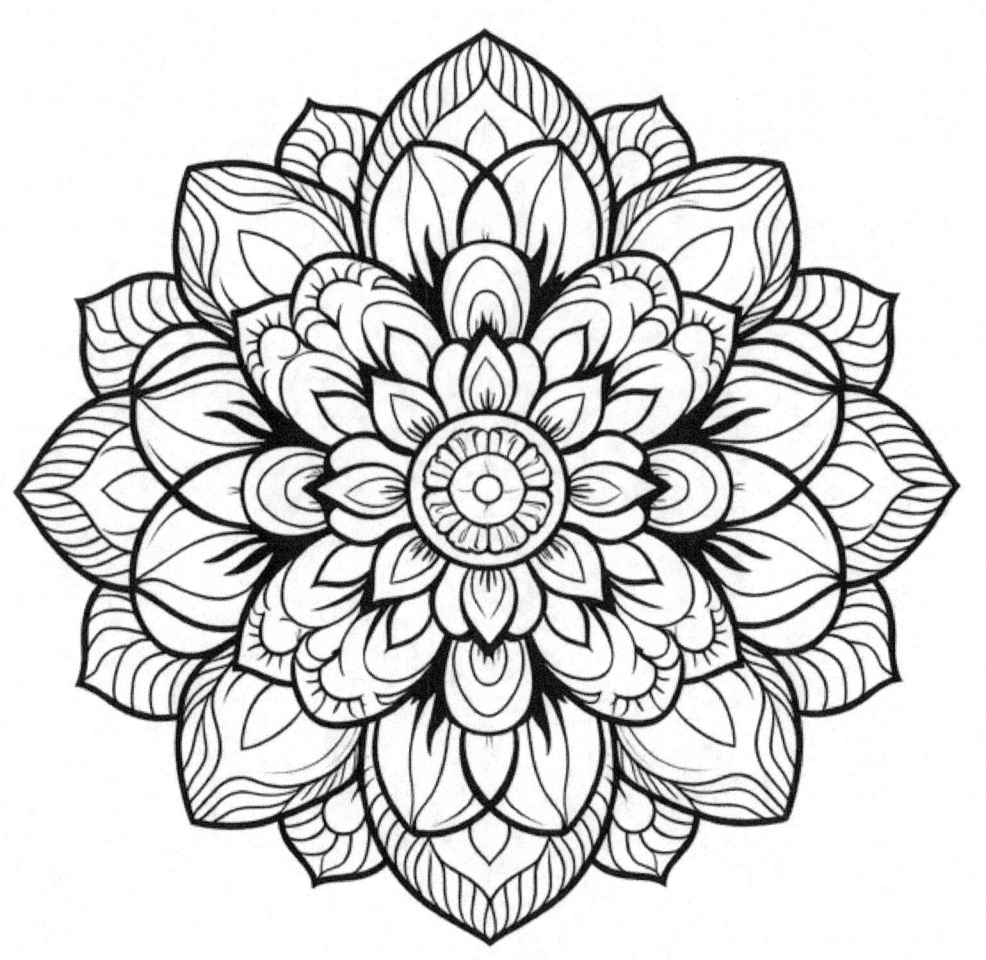

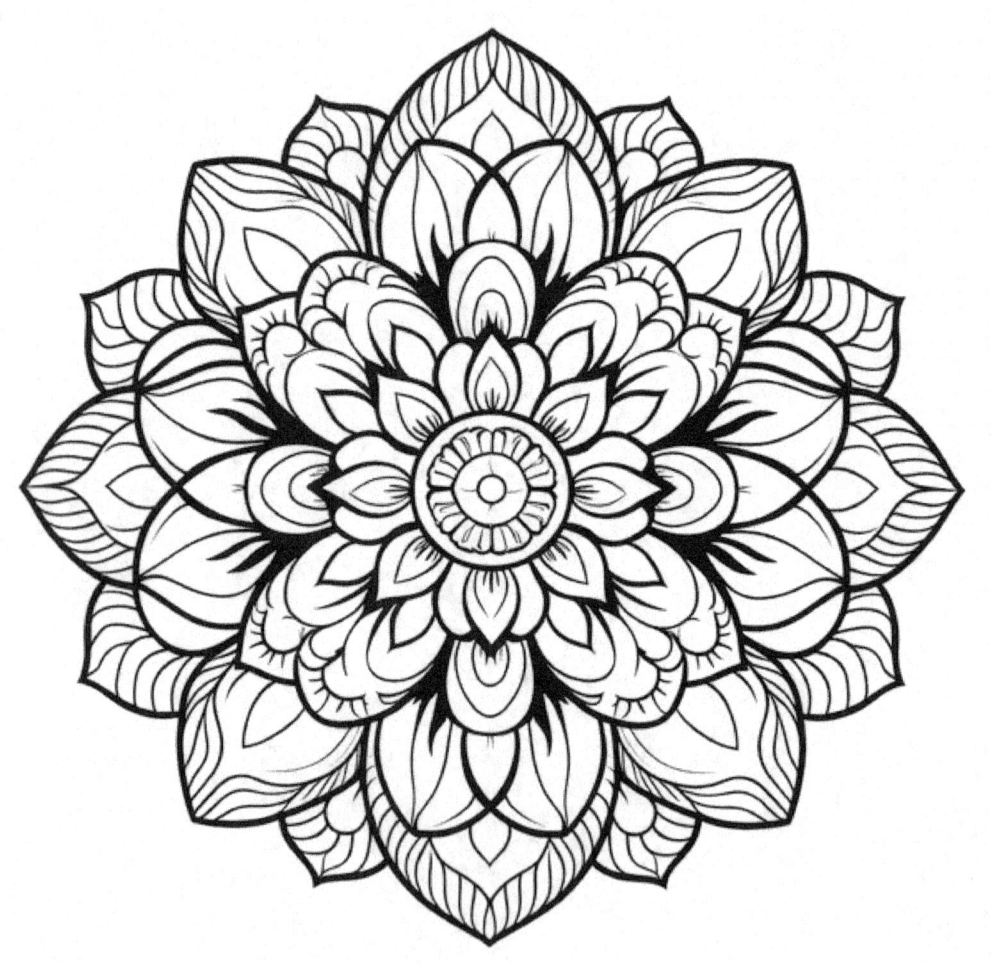

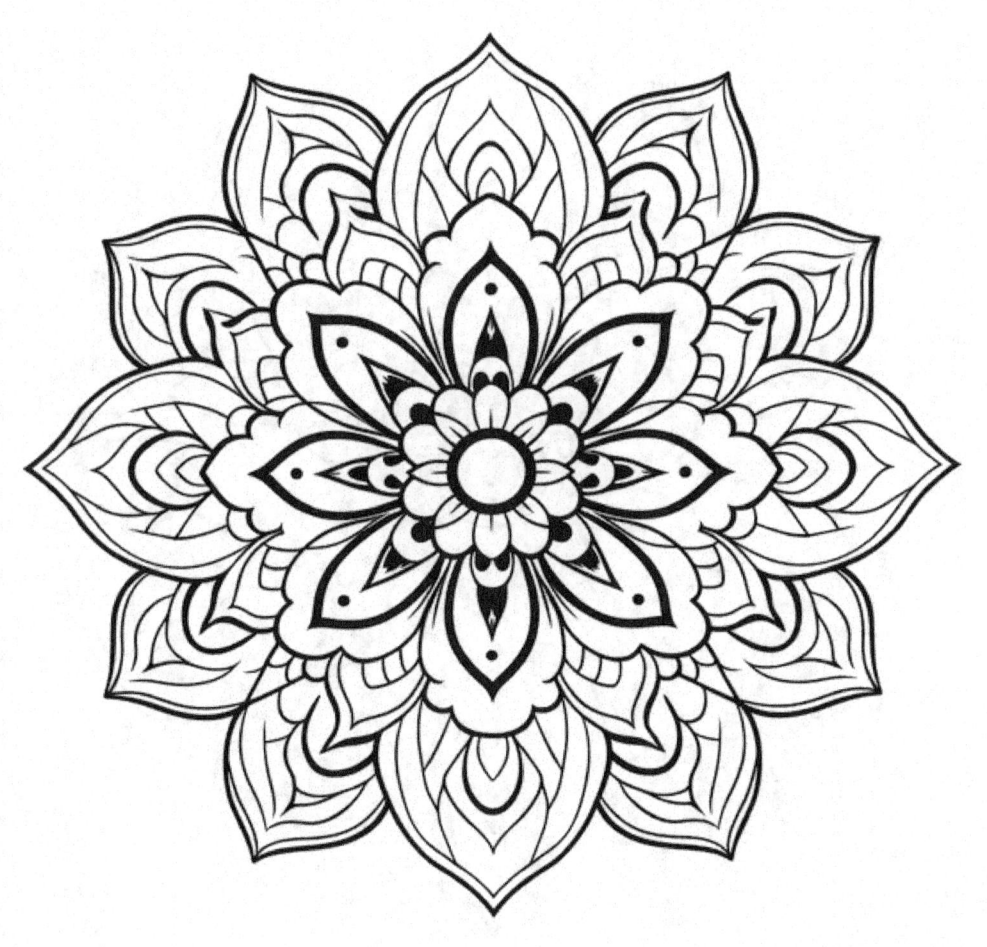

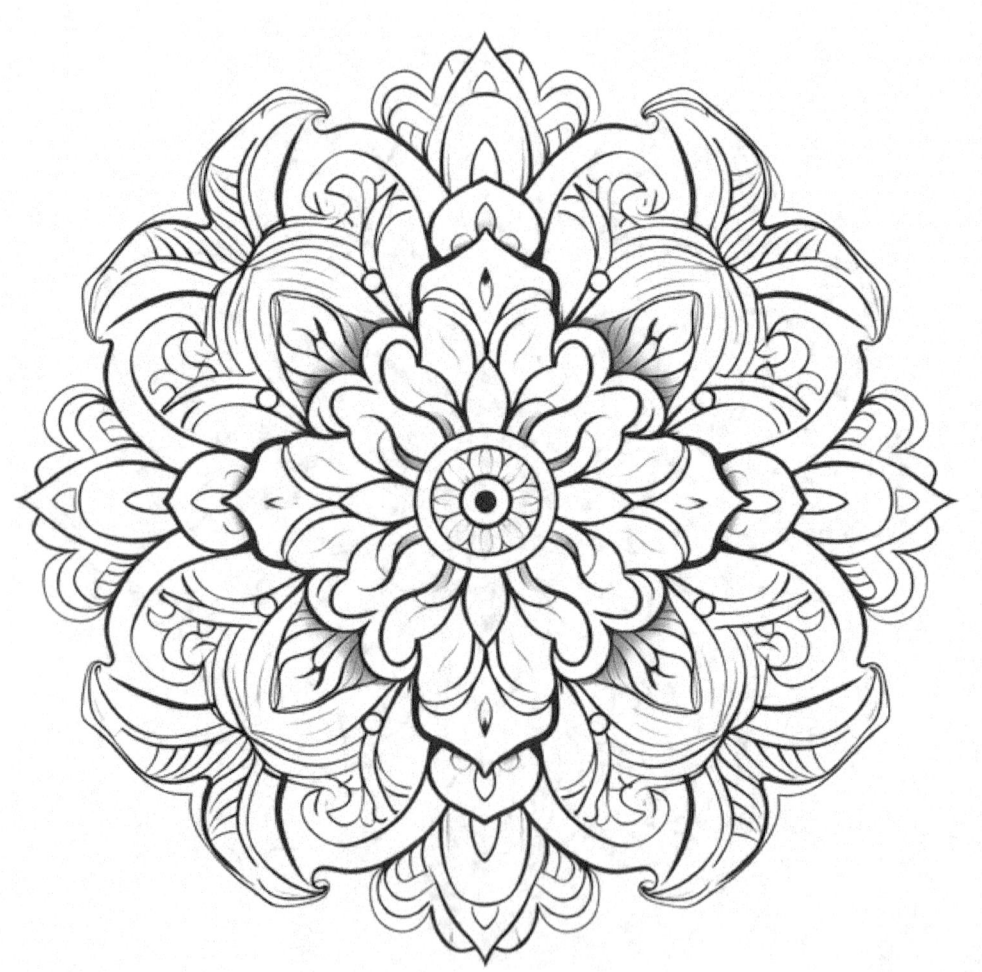

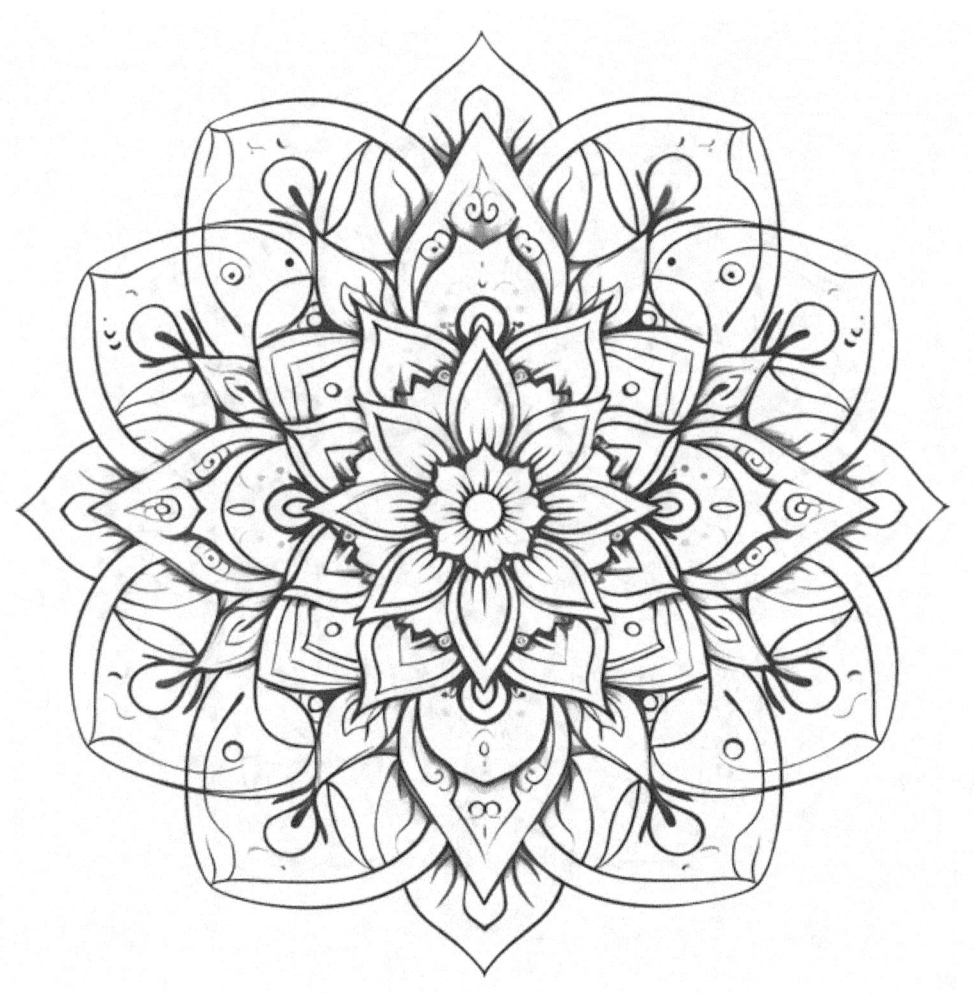

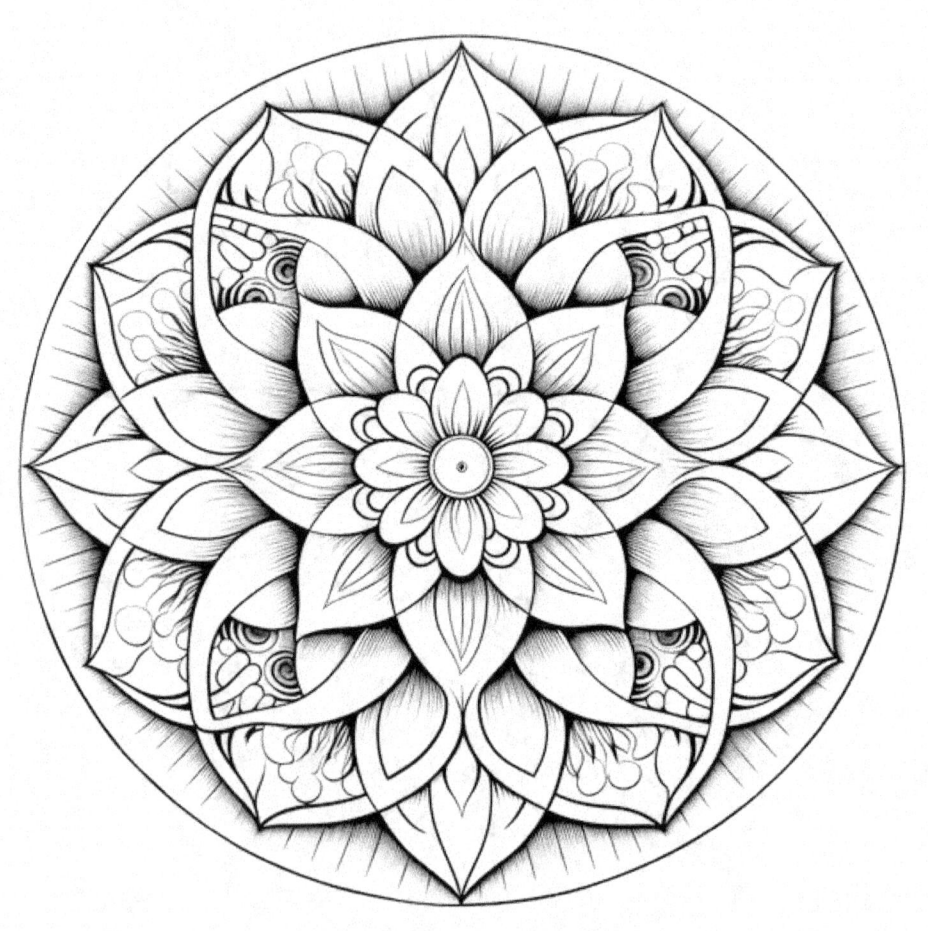

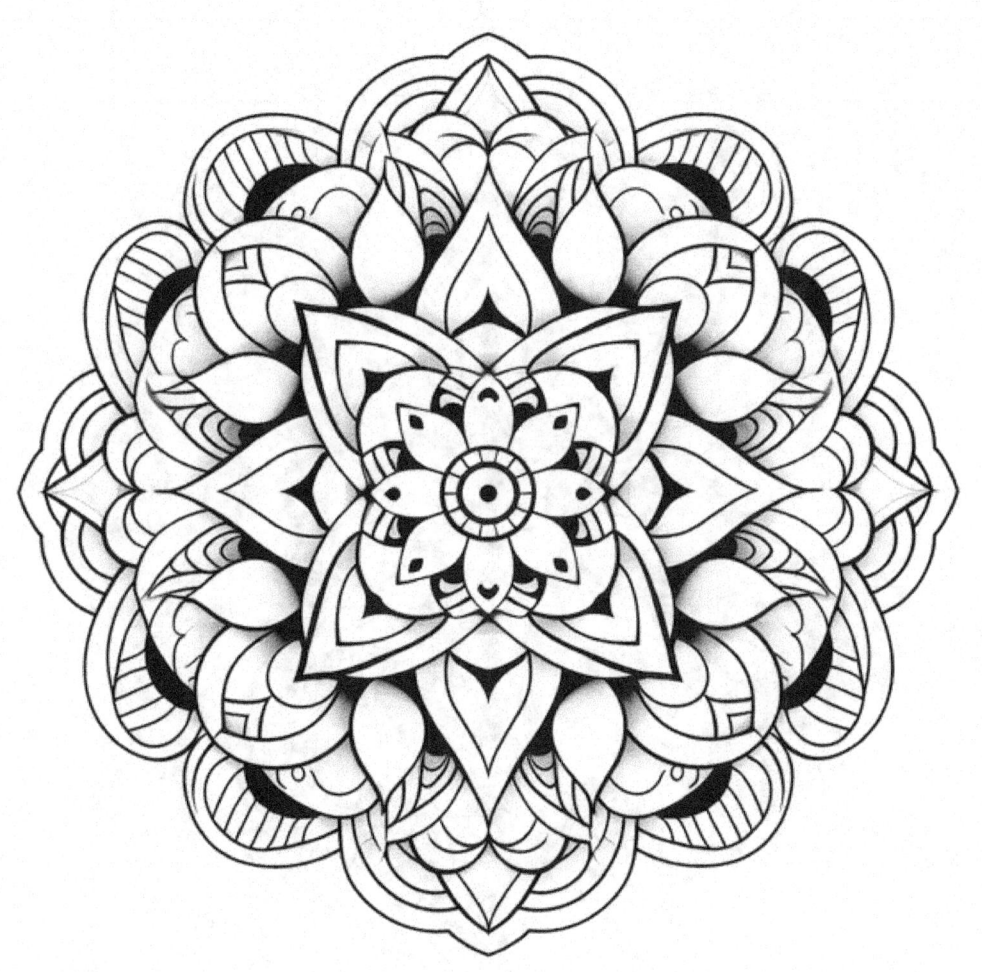

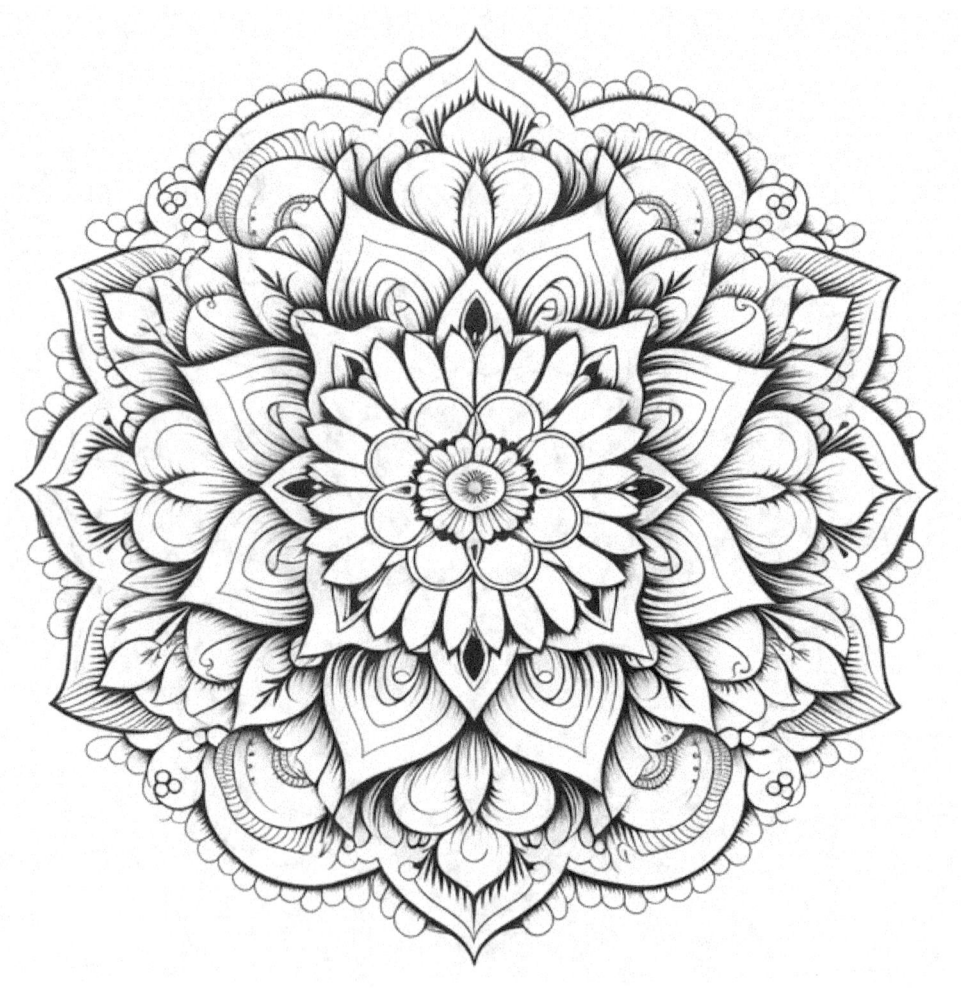

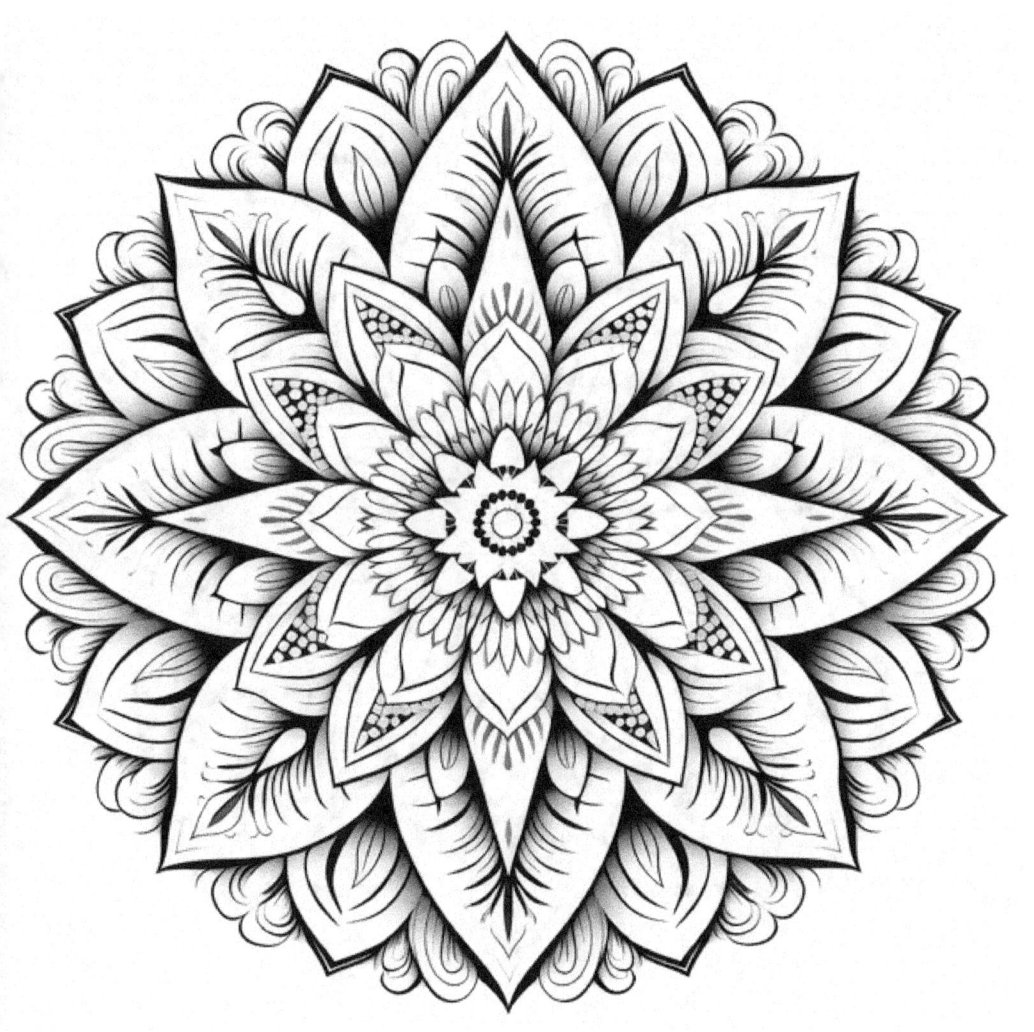

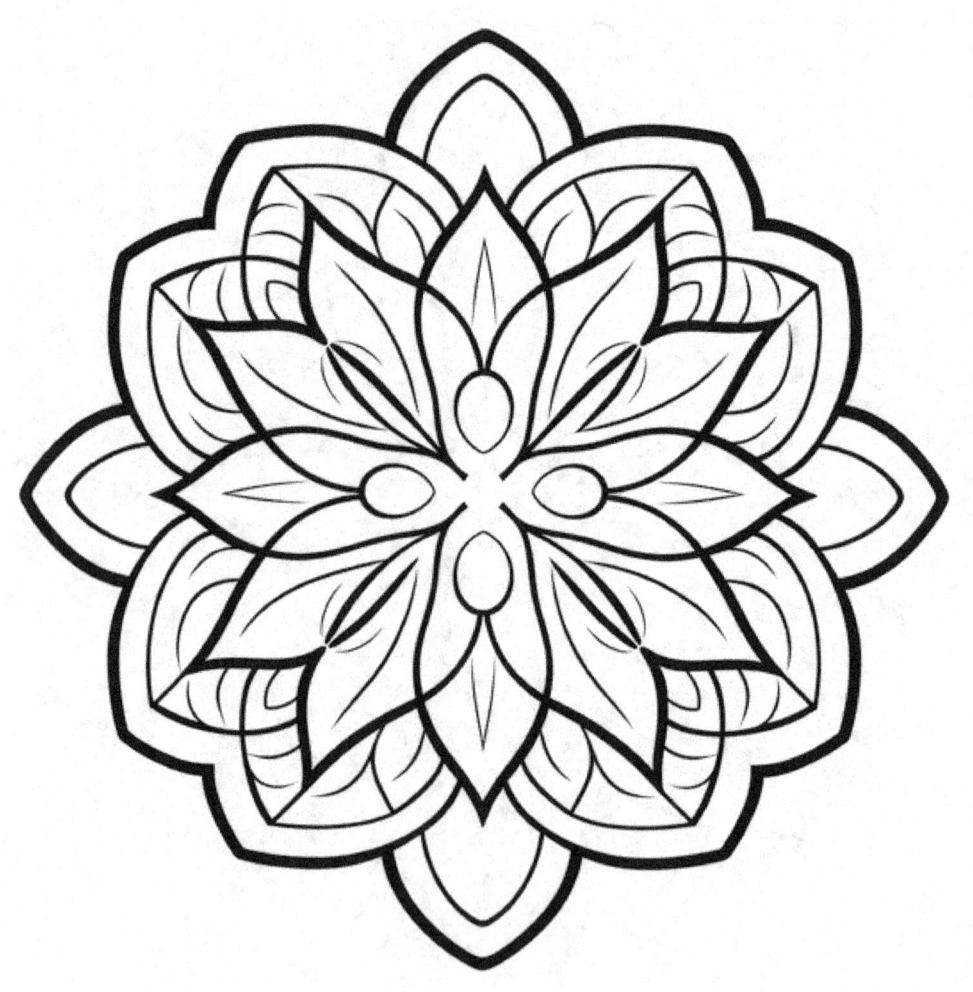

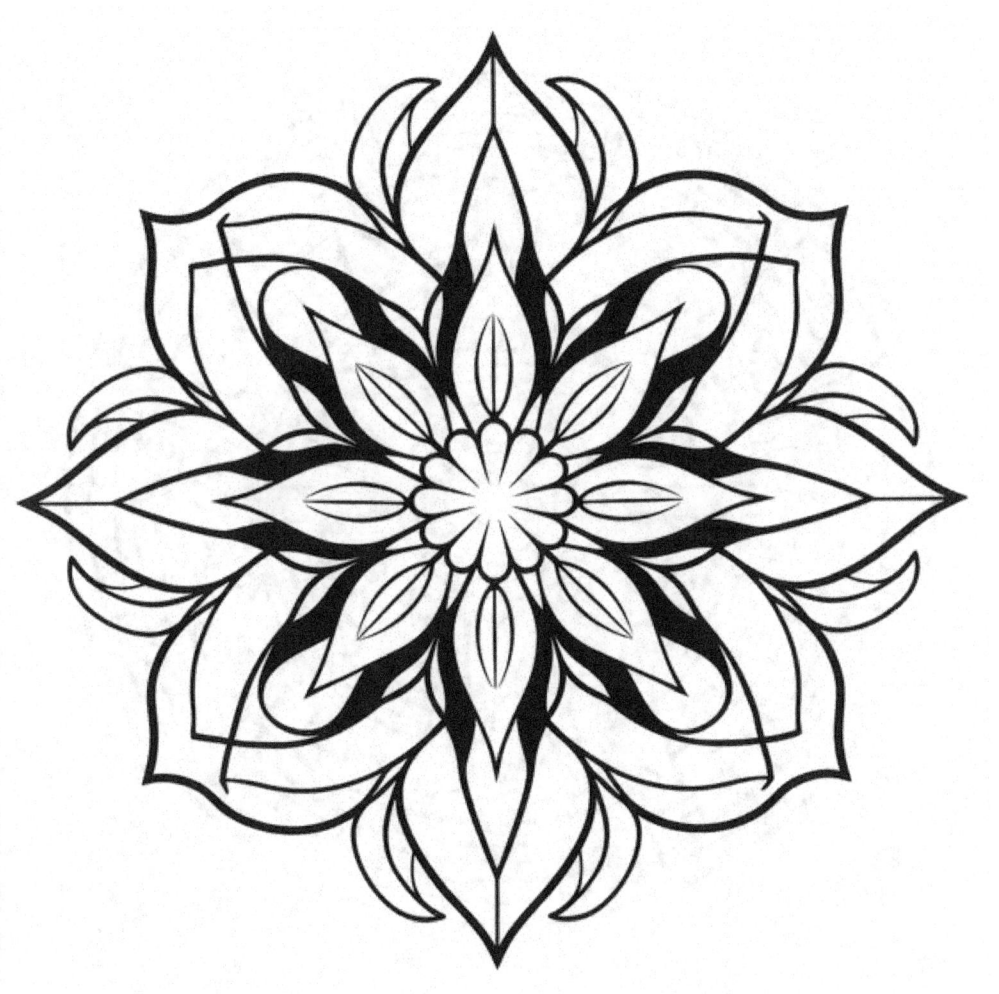

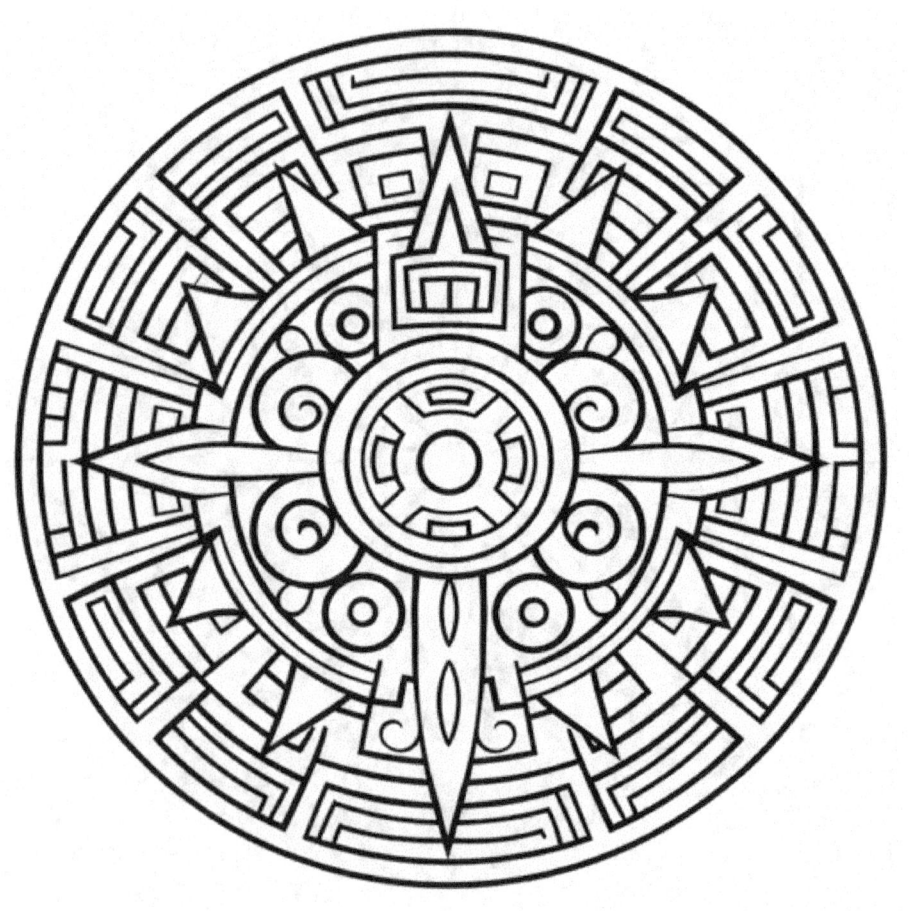

www.ingramcontent.com/pod-product-compliance
Lightning Source LLC
Chambersburg PA
CBHW062301290526
45794CB00006B/2649